Journey Wi

David Bolton was born and educated in
Cambridge, reading English and Law at Sidney
College. He joined the *Liverpool Daily Post
and Liverpool Echo*, spending several years
in their Fleet Street office. He then went into
the public-relations business, heading two
London-based international consultancies and
travelling all over the world. He now works as a
freelance writer on the subject of the English
waterways.

Journey Without End partly duplicates the 1939
route of the legendary *Cressy*, recorded by
L.T.C. Rolt in his classic *Narrow Boat*. Evocative of a past way of life, it will appeal to all who
have ever taken, or dreamed of, a canal holiday.

'Wonderfully evocative.' *Publishing News*

'A gently persuasive travelogue.' *Books*

'A splendid read.'
Inland Waterways Association

David Bolton

Journey Without End

A Voyage through England's Waterways

With illustrations by John Mansbridge

Methuen · Mandarin

A Mandarin Paperback

JOURNEY WITHOUT END

First published in Great Britain 1987
and reprinted 1988
by Methuen London
This edition published 1989
by Methuen · Mandarin
Michelin House, 81 Fulham Road, London SW3 6RB

Mandarin is an imprint of the Octopus Publishing Group

Copyright © 1987 David Bolton
Illustrations copyright © 1987 John Mansbridge

British Library Cataloguing in Publication Data

Bolton, David, *1931–*
  Journey without end : a voyage through
  England's waterways.
  1. England. Inland waterways. Boating –
  Biographies
  I. Title
  797.1′092′4

ISBN 0 7493 0027 2

Printed in Great Britain
by Cox & Wyman Ltd, Reading

To Lynda
without whom none of this
could have been achieved

Contents

Acknowledgements

We wish to thank Eric and Ruth Hunt for their advice, support and friendship, especially during the winter, and Eric for permission to reproduce his poem on p. 87; John Maybank and Penny Dickins for their unfailing collection and delivery of our post; and many other people who gave help and encouragement at one time or another along the way.

We would also like to give grateful thanks for their kind permission to reproduce extracts to Allen Hyman Ltd (*Inland Waterways of England* by L. T. C. Rolt); David and Charles Publishers plc (*Voyage into England* by John Seymour); the Rector of Cogenhoe, Northamptonshire; and the town Council and Chamber of Trade, Bewdley, Worcestershire.

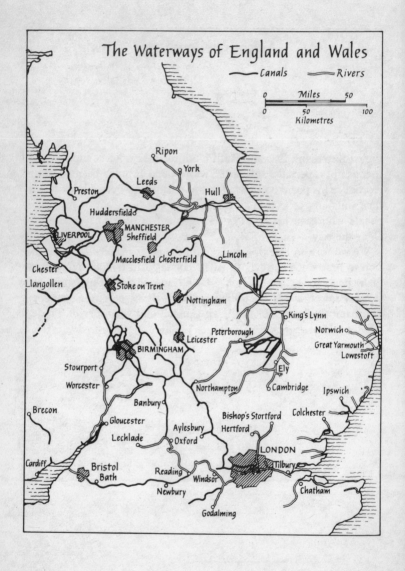

The Waterways of England and Wales

— Canals   — Rivers

Miles
0 ——— 50
0 —— 50 —— 100
Kilometres

Ripon
York
Leeds
Huddersfield   Hull
Preston
LIVERPOOL   MANCHESTER
Sheffield
Chester   Macclesfield Chesterfield
Llangollen   Lincoln
Stoke on Trent
Nottingham
King's Lynn
Peterborough   Norwich
Leicester   Great Yarmouth
BIRMINGHAM   Lowestoft
Stourport   Ely
Worcester   Northampton   Cambridge   Ipswich
Brecon   Banbury
Gloucester   Bishop's Stortford   Colchester
Lechlade   Aylesbury   Hertford
Cardiff   Oxford   LONDON
Bristol   Reading   Tilbury
Bath   Windsor   Chatham
Newbury
Godalming

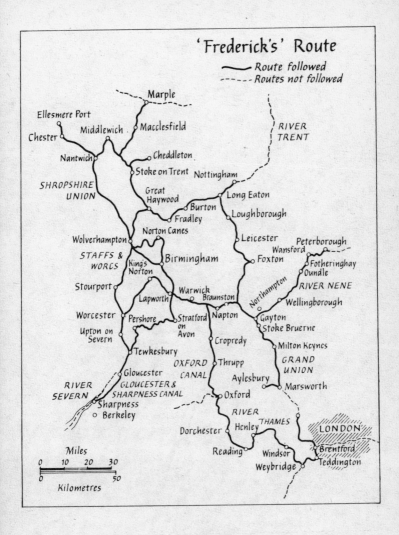

'Frederick's' Route

——— Route followed
- - - - Routes not followed

Return to the start

The last bridge on the canal was so low and long that it was almost like a short tunnel, dark and dank. As the boat approached it, those at the bow end hastily grabbed items from the roof, which barely scraped under the concrete arch, while on the stern the steerer had to crouch so low that he could hardly see ahead. He sounded a long hoot on the horn to warn any oncoming boat and the sound echoed stridently.

At the far end, the chunky black bow emerged into blazing sunlight while, seventy feet behind, the steerer was still lost in the gloom. Then the whole length of the slim, dark-blue narrowboat appeared from under the bridge and the sun momentarily blinded the steerer, who slowed the craft to a halt, shielded his eyes with his hand and studied the scene.

They had emerged into a large, oblong basin. On one side a busy main road carried heavy lines of traffic over the bridge; on the other there was a park of patchy brown grass, burnt dry by the summer sun and trampled by myriads of tourists. Tall trees cast deep, cool pools of shadow where people sat and lounged on the ground.

The rich sound of a band floated on the warm air and brass instruments glinted in the sun; elsewhere could be heard the regular harsh clap and jangle of morris dancers leaping and jumping. A line of multi-coloured national flags, representing many countries, fluttered in front of a substantial red-brick building – the Memorial Theatre and home of the Royal Shakespeare Company. For this was Bancroft basin in the heart of Stratford-on-Avon. The basin – once threatened with closure, saved when the canal had been restored twenty years ago – was lined with boats of all sizes, but there was a place just long enough to take the newly arrived boat opposite the bridge.

Lynda and I – for this was our boat, *Frederick* – hugged with delight, and then clasped the friends who had joined us over the last few miles. We had reached our first goal on the waterways in the boat that was to be our home for more than twelve months.

Behind us were two days of heavy, demanding work descending the Stratford canal. Thirteen miles and thirty-five locks is a fairly formidable undertaking in the best of circumstances, and this particular canal is notorious for its difficulties as a result of past poor maintenance. Added to this, Lynda and I had had relatively little experience so far of handling such a long boat.

Still further behind us, metaphorically, lay an even longer journey which had started five years earlier in Stratford – the place where our romance with the inland waterways was conceived. Now we had returned as we had dreamed, by the long, slow way round from London, instead of dashing there by car.

It had all begun on a fine balmy May evening after we had driven out from London to spend the weekend in Stratford. Walking beside the Avon on our way to a performance in the theatre, we passed a young couple sitting on the bank beside the river drinking champagne with their supper. It looked idyllic.

Later, after an enchanting production of *The Tempest*, that dream play about castaways on a magical island, we left the theatre in the soft dusk as lights were glowing warmly, beckoning from the cabins of the long, narrow and highly decorated boats around the basin. Still held by the play's spell, we wandered slowly past them, talking aloud about them, envying their marvellous mooring, wondering about the inside of the boats, speculating on where they had come from and where they were going.

Little did we realise at the time that our spoken thoughts must have been overheard by many of the occupants, since such discussions can be heard distinctly through the fairly thin skin of these boats. Now, on our return to Stratford, we found that the roles were reversed. Even as we were tying up to the bank, the vanguard of tourists were coming up to admire the fine elegant lines of *Frederick* and ask the same questions that *we* had pondered over.

'That's a big barge,' someone remarked.

'Narrowboat, actually,' I replied. 'So called because it's only seven feet wide – the maximum for many English locks.'

Undeterred, he persisted: 'Have you come far?'

'Well, immediately, over the last two days, just from Lapworth and down the Stratford canal,' I replied. 'But before that we had been moving from Oxford for some weeks.'

He looked surprised. 'Sounds great – how do you manage to have so much holiday?'

'We're living on the boat for a year – a kind of sabbatical,' I explained.

'Living on it, really? You mean all the time?'

'Yes, we're just starting to do that – until two months ago both of us were working in London and living on land. But we got fed up with the rat-race and especially the commuting – strikes, breakdowns, snowbound roads. So we decided to take a year off.'

'Nice if you can afford it,' he grimaced ruefully.

'Probably we can't, but we're giving it a try. It costs less to live on a boat . . .'

'Yes, but how much does a boat like this cost?'

'Well, er, quite a bit, of course.' I hesitated at the directness of the question: no one ever asks a stranger how much his house is worth. 'It's like asking how long is a piece of string. For instance, a shorter boat than this one, say forty-five foot, could cost about £15,000 secondhand and in reasonably good condition; on the other hand, to have a seventy-foot boat built specially for you, fully fitted, could set you back around £40,000. But, again, you could find one in poor condition, needing a lot of work, for a few thousand.'

The man looked questioningly at his companions, presumably his family, and they started to move along; but he was not yet satisfied.

'It sounds a great way of life – how are you finding it?'

'Fantastic, it's like being let out of school,' said Lynda, 'or finishing a prison sentence – not that I know about that!'

'Even so, it's not all fun and no work,' I added. 'In some ways, we've never been busier. For one thing, we're both still doing some freelance work and that takes us back to London every two or three weeks. Then there is always something to be done to the boat – even though it was nearly new when we bought it three months ago, we've since found that the entire exterior has got to be stripped and repainted.'

I glanced along the seemingly endless seventy-foot cabin super-structure and shuddered at the thought of the task that we planned to tackle while moored in Stratford.

'I pity you,' he laughed. 'And after that, where are you going to next?'

'First, down the Avon to Tewkesbury and then back up the Severn to Worcester. Eventually we have to cross over to Braunston in Northamptonshire, where the boat is going into dry dock for the final refitting.'

'And, after that, perhaps York,' added Lynda. 'I've always wanted to go there since two years ago we met a charming American couple doing a year's sabbatical cruise like this, and they were heading to York for the festival just as we had to return to London. I was so envious.'

'You mean to say that you can travel all the way there by boat? Don't you have to take it overland at some point?'

'Not at all. You can go by water in a boat like this from Godalming in Surrey to York in the north, and from Sharpness in Gloucester-shire to Peterborough in the east,' I explained. 'There's an amazing network of canals and rivers which are interconnected – but how far we actually manage to go this year is anyone's guess.'

'So how much does all that cost? Do you have to have a licence?'

'Yes, that's a bit of a problem. Although there is this extensive network, it's not an integrated system. Most of the canals are covered by a single annual licence from BWB – British Waterways Board – though in fact the one we've just come down is run by the National Trust, who make a separate charge. Then, a lot of rivers come under the water authorities and other bodies. For instance, when we pass through the lock over there, out of the basin and on to the Avon, we have to buy another licence – it's not very expensive, but it all adds up.'

'What about other costs?'

'Well, there's diesel for the engine, which provides electricity as well as propulsion; very large gas cylinders for the cooker and the refrigerator; and solid fuel for the stove and hot water – but of course we don't have any gas or electricity bills to pay.'

'And moorings – can you stop where you like or do you have to pay for this?'

'Again, this varies a lot. On the BWB canals there's an understanding that you can tie almost anywhere on the towing-path for up to two weeks in any parish. Rivers, though, can be more tricky: the upper Thames, for instance, has all sorts of lovely places if you like being out in the country, but many of the towns make an overnight charge of £1 or £2.'

By now the rest of the family had drifted away, the wife looking rather bored by the discussion and being tugged on by a lively, but still more indifferent, young Alsatian. The children, a boy and a girl just into their teens, were romping across the park. The man gazed after them speculatively.

'I envy you. It sounds great and I've often thought about a boating holiday, but I doubt if the wife would agree. She prefers to laze on a hot beach around the Mediterranean,' he said sadly. 'Anyway, must go now and I've taken up enough of your time. Thanks anyway, good luck and have a good time.' Then, looking directly at Lynda, 'I hope you get to York.'

We watched him saunter after his party, obviously ruminating on our talk. Beyond, at the far end of the basin, a large crowd was milling on the curved arch of the bridge over the lock, studying a boat that was passing through it. 'Gongoozlers', the old boaters used to call them, and it seems that the fascination of watching a crew work a boat through a lock has never changed.

There is a sense of timelessness about the systematic, disciplined operation of raising or lowering a boat in a lock in order that a level is made with the next section of water. An experienced crew will be seen to be working calmly and unhurriedly, the rate being dictated by the mechanism that controls the flow of water. Yet to the uninitiated it may appear to be a mysterious proceeding, one fraught with difficulties, dangers and hard work.

It was cooler now with the sun starting to drop behind the foliage of the tall trees, but the crowds were as thick and ebullient as ever. A variety of different accents – American, German, French and Japanese – could be distinguished among the other sounds. Tourism, obviously, was big business in Stratford.

We moved inside the cabin and sat with the friends who had helped us over the last arduous stages of the Stratford canal.

Entering from a small open bow cockpit, through a narrow pair of doors, almost half the length of the boat can be seen. The first impression is of the richness and warmth of the wood, as the main cabin walls are lined, unusually, with natural teak which has to be oiled regularly. This has been ingeniously contrasted with darker polished mahogany from waist height to the floor, and the end walls are of light Parana pine. The selection of natural woods throughout the boat was planned by the original owner with such an eye to perfection that he could not bring himself to fix anything to the walls. There were no pictures or light fittings when we took over. We felt that this was carrying things too far, although it did hurt to screw in the first fixtures.

This front section of the boat is open-plan, about thirty feet long, and artfully designed in three sections. First, there is a narrow passage formed by a fitted cupboard on one side and a fixed seat which doubles as a single berth on the other. Next, beyond a low room-divider and on a hearth of natural stone, stands the large solid-fuel Parkray stove which heats both domestic water and central heating.

As the saloon had no furnishings when we bought the boat, we moved a six-foot settee, which opens into a double berth, on board – a feat of physical and mental dexterity which occupied two anxious hours of pushing, pulling, lifting and coaxing. We added a very slim dining-table (which easily seats six with the leaves raised), bookshelves and a nest of tables (inherited from grandparents). Such loose furniture creates a warmer, more homely atmosphere than the fixed seating and tables more commonly found on boats.

This main cabin leads directly into the kitchen, which is about eight feet long, with a central corridor and cupboards and work tops fitted on either side. It is just like any other small kitchen, with a split-level oven, four gas rings, refrigerator, and fully automatic washing-machine.

At this point, the corridor turns to the right with entrances off it to the bathroom (containing a shower and full-size bath) and spare cabin (converted into use as an office). It ends in a large bedroom which has a fitted double berth specially designed twelve inches higher than normal in order to provide storage space beneath and to sit over a projection of the hull. Finally, a door opens into the compact engine-room which has a 46 h.p. Mercedes diesel engine and associated 240V. generator, and from here a sliding hatch gives access to the stern – or counter, as a narrowboat stern is called.

As we sat in the main cabin, people continued to tramp along the path of the Bancroft basin at about window height, giving us an intriguing view of moving legs. Although the large timber-framed windows are double-glazed, we could hear the patter of comments.

'This is a long one, isn't it?'

'Sure, it must be an old working boat that's been converted. It probably used to carry coal around the Midlands.'

'Look at that, George, it's got an automatic washing-machine.'

'And a telly.'

'Gosh, it's even got a bath.'

We looked at each other, smiling – yes, we do actually wash even though we live on a boat. We were pleased at the admiration that *Frederick* was receiving, yet somewhat surprised at the undisguised way in which passers-by think nothing of peering into a boat and openly remarking to each other about its features.

'Perhaps they think we're foreigners and don't understand English,' Lynda suggested.

'In a way I suppose we are – leading such different lives.'

'All the same, it's our home and no one would dream of going up to a house in this way; but, then, boat people are thought to be a race apart. Do you remember Mig and Jim (the first people we met who had lived on a boat for years) telling us how the gypsies camping nearby ordered their children to keep away from "those boat people"?'

Living and travelling on a boat is perhaps the truest Romany lifestyle practised today in Britain since it has a freedom and lack of restrictions no longer found on and around the roads. It is actually possible to keep moving on, and stopping more or less where the fancy takes you, over some 3,500 miles of waterways – the third longest network in Europe after Holland and France. Of course many people who choose to live on boats rarely, if ever, move them. It is simply an alternative, sometimes cheaper, form of housing – though most boatdwellers love the sensation of living on water and enjoy the environment around them.

Our own plan, however, was to travel as much as possible during the twelve months that we had opted out of London life. Although some way off normal retirement age, between us we had been working continuously for over fifty years in the kind of consultancy jobs which soak up nervous energy and cause stress. We felt that we were entitled to have some freedom to enjoy life before it was too late to appreciate it fully.

We wanted to explore the parts of England that had been concealed from us by our city-based working life and to find out what kind of life existed north of Watford – whether the traditional standards of country folk had survived the ever-spreading encroachment of urbanisation, the technological revolution and the crippling decline of older industries. After years of being trampled underfoot on the tube and jostled in Oxford Street, we wished to make a voyage of discovery to see if there was still another England where people cared about the environment in which they lived and were concerned about their neighbours.

It was a year after our first discovery, on that enchanted May evening in Stratford, of narrowboats that we decided – almost on the spur of the moment and without bothering to find out much in advance – to hire a delightful small boat called *Emma* and take a week's holiday on the Llangollen canal.

By chance, we had picked one of Britain's finest routes – one that climbs up the steep valley sides of the Dee high into the Welsh mountains and ends above the sturdy stone town on the edge of the turbulent rushing river. On the way, we passed through Chirk tunnel, 459 yards long, and over the great Pontcysyllte aqueduct, 1,000 feet long with a sheer drop of 120 feet over the Dee. Afterwards we were not certain which had been the most daunting experience, though for me it was probably the aqueduct since I have an appalling head for heights.

What we had discovered was a compellingly attractive way of life, combining the pleasant sensation of living on water with endless opportunities to enjoy the countryside and quaint villages we passed through. We found that being on a boat has its own indefinable allure as you feel it gently rock under your feet in response to any movement on board or from passing craft; this feeling is intensified if you are lying in bed in a snug, wooden-lined cabin.

The scenery is constantly changing at a restful pace which enables you to take in details and select at leisure an ideal place for the overnight mooring. We have usually favoured a remote spot in the country with beautiful views and animals in the surrounding fields: their activities provide unceasing entertainment and we have learned a lot from observing their habits.

Water creates a continuously fluctuating backdrop, throwing back reflections from the glassy surface on calm days, waves chuckling against the hull in high winds. We have shared these times with a great variety of waterfowl: noisy, excitable mallards; arrogant, gliding swans; timid, bobbing coots (like white-faced monks in black habits); gregarious flocks of Canada geese; solitary herons. Something is always going on in a water environment.

On other occasions we have tied in the very heart of historic cities: under the great east rose window of Worcester cathedral, opposite Oxford's dreaming spires on Christ Church meadow, and on Henley's Royal Regatta course. In such places we have felt privileged to enjoy the magnificent view from our home, since no one would be allowed to build a house on these sites.

We took a second holiday on another, slightly larger hire boat only three months after our first venture – this time on the other side of the country on the quietly flowing river Nene from Peterborough to Oundle. Then, six months later, on a frosty January day, we bought our own forty-five-foot narrowboat, *Hanover*, which was at that time moored at Godalming on the river Wey.

Over the next four years our initial enthusiasm became an addiction as we spent many weekends and holidays exploring parts of the Grand Union from London to Northamptonshire, and the entire length of the Thames from tidal Brentford to Lechlade in the Cotswolds.

Restricted holidays, however, meant that we were not able to reach the more distant parts of the system. With an average of one lock to every one and a half miles of canal, progress can be relatively slow; even in a day spending eight hours on the move it would be unusual to travel more than twenty miles, which would normally include some ten to fifteen locks. Many locks are in fairly poor condition, with heavy gates and stiff winding gear, so that with just two of us it can be quite hard work. Even so, we prefer the heavily locked sections to the long, flat pounds between flights; we take it strictly in turn to steer the boat or prepare the locks.

Although some hire boats, with large and strong crews, succeed in completing a ring of canals – perhaps covering 200 miles – in a week, we feel that setting too ambitious a target is the antithesis of what a boating holiday should be. We have taken pleasure in the slow pace (BWB has a maximum speed of 4 m.p.h. on canals and on many shallow, weedy sections it is often not possible to reach even this), enjoying the sights around us and stopping to walk along the towing-path or into neighbouring villages.

These, then, were some of the features of the waterways that attracted us to make a complete change in our way of life, previously structured around a five-day working week, starting early in the morning and frequently not finishing until late into the evening, involving tiresome commuting and all the pressures and intrigues that are an inevitable aspect of competitive businesses.

As the idea started to take root, we talked it over with friends and relatives who reacted in various ways from chiding doubts about whether, in the end, we would take the plunge to advice 'not to be so daft as to give up good jobs when there's so much unemployment around'. Others were envious of the long, leisurely summer days we would spend but anxious about our living on a boat through the winter. 'Won't it be too cold, living on water?' 'What will you do when the canal is frozen over?' The consensus was that we would tire of it quickly.

When we decided to make the break – and the day came when Lynda resigned her job – it all seemed rather daunting. Even though we were planning to do nothing as challenging and dangerous as sailing across oceans, it was an adventure to us – especially as neither Lynda nor I had lived outside the confines of a town before.

Changing over from one lifestyle to another was enormously demanding and time-consuming. We had to find a tenant for our new town-house in Islington, only a mile from the Barbican in the City of London, and we discovered that renting your home is a more emotional step than selling since you are inviting a stranger to share your possessions. We had to round off our work, nothing like as easy as we had expected – and at this time it became apparent that some clients wished us to continue on a freelance basis.

We had to look for another, larger boat as we felt that *Hanover* would be too cramped as our only home, though we were very sad to sell it. Having found the new boat, we had to start furnishing and equipping it. We also had to make arrangements for redirecting the mail. The one thing we did not succeed in doing was selling the car, as intended, since it was needed right up to the time that we moved our personal belongings from the house on to *Frederick*, and then there never seemed time or opportunity to dispose of it. In any case, how do you go about selling a car when you have no fixed address and telephone?

We found, in fact, that dropping out is hard work.

Now that we had arrived in Stratford, there was still more hard work of a real physical kind ahead of us. We planned to stay there for two or three weeks and tackle the complete repainting of the cabin exterior. Although *Frederick* had been built only three years earlier – and so little used by the previous owner that it was almost brand new – the paint was flaking badly. Initial attempts at patching had proved useless and we had been advised to take off the existing surface and start again. The trouble appeared to be that the fibreglass skin, providing a watertight seal over the wooden super-structure, had not been correctly treated – etched is the technical term – before the paint was applied. Consequently, the top surface was lifting and splintering.

This was a task for which we had not bargained in setting out on our travels, and I was particularly depressed at the prospect since my previous limited experience of paint-stripping had not been successful. In the end, our worst fears were confirmed. We used gallons of the strongest paint-stripper and scraped and scraped for hour after hour, not helped by a period of intense hot weather. There is an awful lot of surface in the two sides and roof of a seventy-foot boat, even though it is only seven feet wide.

On the other hand, we had the compensation of working in an attractive environment where endless amusement was provided by rowing boats on the river and frequent encouragement from passers-by. We moored immediately opposite the stage door of the Memorial Theatre and became trained talent-spotters. We rewarded ourselves with several visits to see the company in an outstanding season of plays.

All of this lay ahead, however, as we settled in on the first evening in Stratford. The sun had dropped behind the theatre and, as though the stage lights had been switched on, the clear sky flushed with a crimson sunset. The brass band trumpeted to a frenzied crescendo and the morris dancers clapped and jangled to an exhausted climax. The parties of schoolchildren were gathered and counted by weary, anxious teachers; loving couples unwound from each other on the grass; dogs were chased and put on a lead. The girls in short shorts and the boys in tee shirts straggled away to the pubs, while early-comers in smart suits and dresses arrived for that evening's performance.

Sipping wine in the bow compartment, we watched the scene indolently, satisfied that we had achieved our first target of reaching Stratford by boat. We looked forward with keen anticipation to the coming weeks when, once the paintwork had been finished, we would be free to continue our journey and explore new waters: down the Avon to Tewkesbury and back up the Severn through Worcester, returning through Lapworth on the way to Braunston – that mecca of narrowboats – where *Frederick* was booked into a dry dock for the final stages of its face-lift.

Chapter One

The drought drives us eastwards

On the first Friday of August, six weeks after our arrival into the Bancroft basin, we were toiling through the series of twenty-two locks that lie between Leamington Spa and Braunston. In order to reach the dry dock before the staff left work at 5 p.m. we had risen at first light as the sun's tentative rays started to pierce the swirling early morning mist and – a rare experience for us – we were the first boat on the move. A pair of former working narrowboats, their holds tented over in traditional green canvas and converted now to use as youth camping craft, had tied above us the previous evening, and one of the crew broke off his morning shave in the open to give us a cheery wave on our way.

The locks on this section of the Grand Union fall into three flights: a group of eight close together at Stockton, four at Bascote and three at Calcutt. At Bascote, we were greeted by the unusual sight these days of a lockkeeper in attendance, dressed in the standard smart blue BWB overalls. Apart from a few special cases, locks on the smaller Midlands canals no longer have a keeper present and boaters are free to work through at any time.

His presence confirmed the rumours we had been hearing from other boaters along the route that British Waterways Board was posting men at certain key locks to control the flow of traffic using them because there was increasing concern about water shortage. This was our first encounter with the situation. The past six weeks had been dry; indeed, there had been little heavy rain for some months so that boatyard staff were gloomily predicting that BWB would not be able to cope with the summer peak of activity without closing some canals. The level of reservoirs had fallen to an all-time low, so to conserve remaining water supplies the use of important flights of locks was being restricted to certain hours each day and boats were being encouraged to pass through in convoys.

In these conditions, as we continued towards Braunston, I wondered why I had gone to the expense of booking four days in the dry dock: two would have sufficed for inspecting, cleaning and painting the hull, the other two days had been reserved only to provide covered conditions for professional sign-writing and decorative painting. For the former, the dry dock was of course essential, but the latter could have been carried out in dry weather in the open.

On the final approach into Braunston there was a straight and wide section of the Grand Union. Ahead, the jagged tooth-edged spire of the church, standing on a promontory, was silhouetted against the clear sky, while the village was hidden in the valley. Like a lighthouse for mariners, it was a welcome sight for Lynda and me – who had travelled from Lapworth over the past two days, covering twenty-seven miles and forty-six locks – and a temporary journey's end where we would spend about a week.

For the working boaters of fifty or more years ago, when the canal would have been congested with pairs of deeply loaded narrowboats, it must have been an even more rewarding prospect. Braunston, at the crossroads of the Oxford and Grand Union canals, was a favoured overnight stop with all the required facilities for feeding and stabling horses, and more recently for fuelling and repairing engines. Unlike us, however, the old boatman on his great traffic run from Birmingham to London – 137 miles and 166 locks accomplished often in less than three days – would probably be arriving after dark and seeking an advantageous mooring below the locks so that he was tactically placed to move off in the morning ahead of competitors.

At the end of the long straight section, two elegant Horsley iron bridges cross over an island at the junction of the canals. To the left, the North Oxford continues towards Rugby, thereafter linking with the Coventry and thence providing a through route to the Trent and Mersey, opening up the north of England. We made a sharp turn to the right under one of the bridges along the Grand Union and into the village.

There were many boats – both old and modern – tied along the side of the canal here, as always in this most popular of boating centres. *Hanover* had been based here up to the time that we sold it, so we looked out eagerly to see which boats we recognised. We chugged slowly past *Valentine* with its curious pointed windows, the romantic though troublesome wooden-hulled *Clevanda*, and then spotted *Poacher* – the modern seventy-foot boat which is the home of Arthur Bray, one of the most revered former working boaters, now in his eighties and still living on water.

We passed the entrance to the marina, packed with cruisers strung out in lines along pontoons. Opposite, the hill rose steeply through fields containing a scattered assortment of cattle, sheep, donkeys, goats, ducks and chickens to the village main street running along the top.

We idled past lines of Union Canal Carriers narrowboats, paired together, their great black hulls sheeted over by green tarpaulin from the diamond-patterned front cratch to the little stern cabin, once the home of large boating families, with plumes of acrid black smoke emerging from the polished brass-bound chimneys. Used today as youth camping boats, the crews were busy loading cases of milk, bread, baked beans, sugar and other supplies for the coming week's trip.

Ahead, the tall, smokey-red, brick chimney of the old steam pumping-house pinpointed the bottom lock of the Braunston flight. Immediately above it to the left was the dry dock within a wide, squat, brick building with a pitched slate roof.

With help from one of the yard's staff we ascended through the lock and out of it, and then reversed back into the dock building. As *Frederick* was not due to be dropped into the dry dock itself until Monday morning, we tied half in and half out of the covered building so that we could enjoy the fine evening light and the pleasant view of the valley narrowing towards the next lock.

As we settled into this curiously unfamiliar situation, with the boat floating half entombed within the building, the westward sky began to fill with threatening clouds and there were distant rumbles of thunder. Soon the smooth surface of the water was broken by the first raindrops. By nightfall, rain was hammering steadily on the exposed part of the cabin, gurgling down the drainpipes and plopping through leaks in the tiles. A long and heavy summer storm continued through much of the night.

'At least I feel better about having booked the dock,' I said to Lynda as we turned in. 'Just imagine if we had risked Ron doing the painting from a mooring on the canalside . . .'

Part of the appeal and fascination of English canals for the many, many people who wander around them stems from the ornate decoration and brilliant colouring of narrowboats – a welcome contrast to the drabness of urban surroundings, an enchanting reminder of traditional styles and skills and an evocative glimpse of the wandering gypsy way of life.

While there are significant regional variations in the character of narrowboat decoration, depending on the whims of the owners and the style of the craftsmen, the traditions established in Braunston over the last hundred years by William Nurser and his son Frank contain most of the features common to other places, such as the ornate fairground lettering, variegated diamond patterns, and the romantic pictures of castles and roses. Their skills have been acknowledged by many to epitomise the finest achievements of the craft.

Ron Hough is one of the few genuine craftsmen who has carried through this tradition in direct line and without a break. Having lived all of his life in Braunston, he trained under the Nursers when Samuel Barlow still had a great carrying fleet based at the marina we had passed; it was subsequently taken over by Willow Wren, the last post-war attempt to find a way of maintaining commercial carriage on the Midland canals.

Ron arrived at the dock on Saturday morning. Now a softly spoken, good-looking man of middle age, he retains a boyhood enthusiasm for Northamptonshire cricket and obviously gains immense satisfaction from the quality of his work. There was great relief when he inspected the boat and pronounced our exterior repainting successful. He believed that we had solved the problem of the flaking surface and that the new paintwork would last through the coming winter, with another top coat to be applied in the following summer.

The original colour scheme had been very dark navy-blue cabin sides and a white roof. We had stayed close to this, though using a somewhat lighter, Oxford blue on the sides, which enhanced the varnished wooden windows. Reflection from the roof had tended to dazzle the steerer on sunny days so we had changed this to a deep red, carrying this colour through on to the stern cabin and counter.

Large panels had been left in undercoat grey on either side of the stern cabin where there were no windows, and similar, smaller panels on the bow. It was here that Ron was to use his art in painting the name, but first we had to agree the style of lettering and embellishment with him. We wanted to create a dramatic yet simple effect and showed Ron a photograph of another boat decorated on the lines we had in mind.

He set to work with chalk to sketch out the shape of the design, using, as his only aid, a flexible strip of wood as a guide to the curved angle of the word *Frederick*. The rest of the design was accomplished entirely in free-hand.

'It's no good measuring the size of the letters,' he explained. 'Each letter has its own dimension according to its character and relative to the style of the whole word. The right aesthetic appearance depends on an overall balance rather than exact measurement.' He illustrated this technique by pointing to other boats where each letter had been drawn to identical size, and the result appeared out of proportion and inelegant.

There was momentary consternation when Ron queried the spelling of the name. Was there a middle 'E' or not? We hurried to find a reference and confirmed that there was. Ron recalled a recent case where a customer had demanded completion of the work in a rush, only to discover that he had supplied a faulty spelling of the name.

As the name panels gradually took shape over the four days, Ron also turned his attention to the stern of the cabin. First, traditional sweeping curves, almost like an Arab window, of red and blue broken by a white line were added to the exterior. Then, much to our delight, Ron suggested decorating the inside of the pair of doors with roses and castles. Up to this point I had worked closely with him, a very rewarding experience, in discussing what I wanted in the way of design. Now Ron came into his own specialist field and took over completely.

Heir to the medieval traditions of painting murals on a working surface, he arrived with a palette and range of oil paints and brushes that would have done credit to Michelangelo, and sat completely absorbed, almost as though in a trance, as he added layer upon layer of colour, bringing fantasy scenes to life. First, a lake of pale azure merging into a lighter sky flecked with darker clouds; then, a landscape upon which rose the round turrets and battlements of a castle, more akin to the fairytale buildings of the Rhine than to English fortresses. Trees, with long upward fronds like palms, sprouted from the land, and boats with wide-arced oriental sails crossed the water.

The picture on each door was composed free-hand and emerged slightly different from the other. Below each one, wide sweeping strokes of red, pink and white blossomed into the petals of roses in full bloom while at the top and bottom of the cascade were stylised, cogwheel-shaped daisies. Sitting or crouched on one knee in the confined space, often with a brush clasped in his mouth while with another he mixed colours on the palette or gently stroked the shapes, Ron worked with utter absorption and obvious delight for some hours.

A small cluster of roses was added to the name on the bow and the job was finished. The three of us stood back to admire the work. *Frederick* at last, after two months of effort, proudly bore his name in the place of ugly blank panels and wore a handsome coat of colours.

Not all narrowboats in the past were given this decoration. Many of the large commercial fleets were allowed no more than the company's name and a number, even though these were often painted in ornate style. Day boats, such as the Joey boats of the BCN (Birmingham Canal Navigation) which were used just for work, had only a number. It was the pairs of boats – a motor, once diesel engines were installed, and an unpowered butty – run by owner captains, the Number Ones, that enjoyed full decoration since this was home to the family as well as the place of work.

There are many theories about the source of this traditional narrowboat painting, but not one seems to provide an entirely acceptable answer. Even Ron cannot explain the tradition that he learned and carries on today.

L.T.C. Rolt in his classic book *The Inland Waterways of England* (Allen and Unwin, 1950), written during the collapse of commercial traffic and the advent of leisure boating, saw a distinct comparison between the beautifully planned boatman's cabin, where every inch of the nine-by-seven-foot living space was cleverly utilised by built-in fold-away furniture, and the traditional gypsy caravan. He believed that the gypsies employed as casual labour by James Brindley in cutting Britain's first industrial canal, the Bridgewater, had subsequently gone on to crew the boats. Yet even he admitted that there was no clear connection with the decorative style of the boats. 'While they undoubtedly betray the gypsy love of bright primary colours, the canal boatman has made these particular forms of decoration peculiarly his own and you may look in vain for roses and castles in the modern gypsy's wagon.'

The nearest equivalent, he felt, could be found in the cart, brightly painted with fanciful flowers, of the Balkan peasants. He put forward the hypothesis that there could have been a tribe of Balkan gypsies who brought with them 'the tradition of flowers and the recollection of the fairy-tale castles of Eastern Europe.'

Other theories suggest a connection with the floral pattern of the china which the original boat people hung on their cabin walls and with the inlaid marquetry of Victorian furniture. Yet no one has produced a wholly convincing explanation of the origins of this widespread cult which can be traced back to the middle of the last century.

Perhaps the answer to this unsolved mystery which fascinates today's boater and industrial archaeologist is that there is no single answer. In their natural desire to embellish their confined living quarters, the untrained folk painters would have sought guidance and ideas from sources around them, including the places through which they travelled. The time coincides with the period when architects were employed to turn the great castles such as Windsor and Arundel, no longer needed as fortresses, into more attractive residences, while some wealthy Victorians indulged their romantic aspirations by constructing mock castles in the Eastern European style. Whatever the explanation, we have benefited by inheriting a unique folk art.

Before Ron Hough reached the final stage of the decoration, *Frederick* had been dropped into the dry dock itself for the more prosaic, though essential work on the hull. It was 8 a.m. on Monday morning when we heard someone throw open the side door and, whistling cheerfully, start crashing around the dock. We were caught still in bed as it was easy to oversleep in the semi-cocooned atmosphere of the rear cabin, protected from daylight, weather and noise by the double skin of the boat and the dock building.

Rapidly throwing on some clothes, I came up on deck, apologetically, to find Gary unconcernedly busying himself with preparations for dropping the boat. *Frederick* was positioned in the centre of the dock and a slim steel plate, the full width of the entrance, was cranked down from above it, providing a seal between the canal and the interior. Then Gary opened a sluice at the rear of the dock, releasing the water into the canal below.

The boat gradually started to lower with the level of the water and some ten minutes later was sitting on lines of beams near the bottom of the dock. Being flat-bottomed and built of steel, a narrowboat can be positioned easily in this manner, the only problem being to clear the propeller and rudder. I realised that a dry dock is really a basic, single-entrance lock in terms of operation.

Our home had become a static island with about five feet clearance all round, so we had to cross from the dock-side on a landing plank. We missed the gentle rocking of the boat on water. The beams on which the hull rested were about four feet from the bottom of the dock, deep in thick, squelching, oozing mud. Dressed in rubber boots and waterproof clothing, Gary climbed down a ladder and started to clean off the hull with a wire brush. It was important not to lose time as the weed clinging to the part of the boat which has been underwater quickly starts to dry and harden.

Similarly geared, I myself descended and walked around the hull with Gary, checking closely to see that there were no signs of undue corrosion or damage. An odd, slightly unreal sensation to see for the first time the whole of the boat, looking ungainly out of water – rather like being able to expose the foundations of the house in which you live. We found an enormous hunk of rope twisted around the propeller shaft, typical of the rubbish picked up from the canals; it was amazing that it had continued to work with this resistance.

The next day, when the hull had thoroughly dried out, it was liberally coated with black bituminous paint which is the standard protection and finish for narrowboats. It meant that for twenty-four hours we could not use waste pipes from the kitchen sink and bathroom, which empty over the side, and had to use buckets instead. Meanwhile, I descended again into the murky depths and, under Ron's watchful eye, painted the two red and white panels on the round stern which, in traditional style, had to terminate in half-moon shapes. The trick of doing this is to apply the colour paint first, and then cut in the shape with black paint.

Over coffee breaks, Gary told us how he had been born on one of the last working boats into a family of fifteen, whose links with the canals went back generations. From an early age he had helped on the boats, and later continued the tradition for a time by running a pair of full-length youth camping boats. When his own family started to arrive, however, they had to move on to land, although his working hours are spent in and around boats. His eyes took on a faraway, distant look as we enthused about our first experiences of living afloat. There are few people who have spent some time living on a boat, and especially those born into it, who do not find difficulty afterwards in adjusting to life on land within four square walls, whatever the reasons may be.

Even though *Frederick* was land-based for a short time, our own life was busy and varied. From the lock outside, Ernie Kendall's strident, authoritarian voice carried into the dock as he cajoled and manoeuvred a never-ending sequence of new hire-boaters for the ascent of the flight. Stepson of Arthur Bray, Ernie has continued the family tradition by living on *Poacher* and working for BWB. He did a magnificent job over this period of drought in grouping boats together and watching keenly for any inefficient lock-handling that could have caused loss of water.

Our friends Simon and Rosemary Grant had recently acquired highly-geared bicycles and these they mounted and rode twenty miles to see *Frederick*'s progress. They have an old, thick-walled stone cottage at the end of a superb line of thatched houses that leads up from the Oxford canal to the church and pub in the historic village of Cropredy, and we have seen them often on our travels in the area. While still in Braunston another violent thunderstorm broke, but this only added to the appeal for Simon and they set off on the return twenty miles in shorts and a torrential downpour.

Soon after they had left on their mad ride, I heard a shout from inside the dock: 'Is David Bolton there?'

I emerged from the cabin, blinking in the gloomy light, and thought that I could make out the shape of Vincent Pearmain. 'Good lord, Vincent, is that you? How did you find me? What are you doing here? Is everything all right?' I exclaimed in rapid succession. Then added, 'Marvellous to see you!'

I had seen him last about two months earlier when, on board *Frederick*, then moored at Thrupp on the Oxford canal, we had concluded some lengthy negotiations and he had purchased *Hanover*. Naturally, a first instinct was to fear that some unexpected problem had arisen with my former boat.

It turned out to be one of those extraordinary coincidences. That very same day Vincent had brought *Hanover* back down the north Oxford canal from Rugby, where the exterior had been completely repainted, and it was now moored in the adjoining yard before being moved to its new base at Tile Mill on the Kennet and Avon canal near Reading. With a total change of colour scheme, we felt that it was somehow not the same boat that had brought us so much pleasure, but Vincent was delighted with the result.

We had a succession of other visitors who were keen to see *Frederick*'s transformation, so that the time in dry dock passed rapidly. Tuesday evening arrived and *Frederick* had shed the last of his interim, awkward skin; he had changed from a slightly ugly duckling into a beautiful swan gleaming with a brand new surface from stem to stern, hull to cabin. The guillotine gate of the dock was lifted slowly, the water started to seep back in and once again he was a floating home.

The next morning was bright and clear as I climbed up the hillside from the dock through wet dew on the field, crushing the grass under polished black leather shoes, clambering the stile in a dark city suit, shirt and tie, now uncomfortable and unfamiliar. Briefcase under arm, I waited for the taxi at the post office. For today, of all days, I had to return to London to attend to some business.

Arriving slightly late, the driver made up for lost time, haring at breakneck speed along twisting, narrow lanes, up and down hill, through the rolling Northamptonshire countryside basking in early morning sunshine. He deposited me five miles away at Long Buckby railway station which stood on stilts high above the golden cornfields, nearly ready for harvesting; there was hardly a house in sight. It seemed to be one of the most isolated and beautifully situated of BR's stations, and it was difficult to believe that a train would arrive to transport me direct from this idyllic spot to Euston in the centre of London's commuterland.

Meanwhile, Lynda, with some trepidation, had been left in charge of bringing the immaculately painted boat out of the dock. It was not going to be a simple manoeuvre since there was insufficient room to turn – or wind – a seventy-foot boat. A semi-derelict barge partially obstructed the passage just outside the dock, so that *Frederick* had to be eased past, reversed into the lock, dropped through it and then steered backwards for 100 yards of congested canal to the first wide point. Narrowboats with a single screw and rudder at the stern are difficult to control in reverse, since the length of the hull tends to swing the bow in one direction or the other against the desired course.

When eventually I stumbled on board at 10 p.m. that evening, battered from travelling and urban encounters, I heard that it had been a somewhat hair-raising experience. As Lynda edged the boat back into the lock, the round stern hit the side and gashed the new white paint. Horrorstruck, Gary came on board to help her and immediately advised her to cover the damage before it was discovered.

Then, with experience learned from the cradle onwards, he gave Lynda a lesson in how to reverse a narrowboat. The art is to alternate the gears between reverse and forward, driving the boat backwards until it is about to go out of alignment, then giving a sharp forward burst to correct the angle of the bows before going into reverse again. Stage by stage the boat is moved backwards without losing the line of direction. Up until then, we had laboriously used shafts at the bow and stern to correct the angle.

The small scrape in the paintwork had not been covered. It had been retained to demonstrate the morning's difficulties and to explain how Lynda had come to learn a new handling technique from an expert. She was now keen to show me this at the earliest opportunity.

The next day it was my turn to make a mistake, also affecting the new paintwork. To protect the sign-writing from scratching and severe weather, it is the practice to cover it with several thin layers of varnish. Ron had left this task to me and I had purchased from one of the big new DIY supermarkets a large can described as 'yacht varnish'. This seemed to be appropriate for the job.

When I started to apply it, however, I found that it was viscous, slightly yellow and difficult to spread evenly with a brush. Being keen to finish this last stage, I foolishly persisted and the brilliant white lettering disappeared under an opaque, sickly pallor. By the time I had covered both sides I realised that I had made a tragic error – the varnish had clearly been of inferior quality.

To celebrate the completion of work, we had invited Ron and his wife on board that evening for a glass of wine. He appeared, tugged along the towing-path by an energetic, tempestuous Airedale, while I stood in front of the side panel hoping to hide my mistake.

His eyes were far too sharp. He looked askance at my handiwork and I confessed to my error. But he reacted kindly, by apologising for not advising me to use the highest-quality varnish. 'Let it weather this winter,' he suggested. 'Then it should be all right.'

The damage, in fact, was not as far-reaching as I had thought: the varnish merely took off the extreme brightness, giving an impression of slight weathering. It did not affect the reaction of walkers on the towing-path in Braunston who stopped frequently to admire and praise. 'What a lovely boat,' one man exclaimed at the bow. Then, on reaching the middle, he said more firmly, 'It's a lovely boat.' Finally he walked to the stern and pronounced, 'It *really* is a lovely boat.'

That was the moment when we could appreciate that all our efforts over the past two months – stripping, scraping, undercoating, painting, dry-docking and more painting – had been enormously worth while. Never before had I felt so proud about any project that I had undertaken, and I realised the deep satisfaction that comes from hard physical work and a job that is well done.

It helped us to understand how it is that wherever there are boats moored or docked people seem to be working endlessly on

them. It is true, as people say, that you never finish working on a
boat.

Our task completed, we set out eastwards towards the river Nene –
where on our second hire-boat holiday the idea, at first remote and
fanciful, of living afloat had taken root. Our original plan for the
rest of this summer had been to return to Oxford and cruise the
Thames to Lechlade, which had been a favourite spot two years
earlier on *Hanover*. However, this meant going down the Oxford
canal, which is congested at peak times and can be notoriously
shallow in the best of years. Rumours that the drought conditions
were worsening decided us against this course. The Nene was likely
to guarantee us better boating conditions, while after the past busy
and active weeks we felt that we would find quiet and peace on the
little-used river.

The Nene is one of the least well known of the great English
rivers, undeservedly so. It is the classic willow-banked river,
winding endlessly through rich watermeadows, past old mills and
skirting historic stone-built villages. Rising in the East Midlands
uplands, it provides the major drainage channel through to the
Wash, so that guidebooks warn about its proneness to flooding.
This, we felt, would not affect us this year.

On the canal, BWB was continuing its policy of saving water by
pairing up boats passing through broadbeam locks whenever possible. The Grand Union locks, such as the six on the lovely Braunston
flight, were designed to accommodate comfortably side by side two
narrowboats of less than seven feet in width, and up to seventy-two
feet in length. Originally, this facilitated the progress of a pair of
working boats, the motor and its butty, and this was achieved on a
flight (where locks are grouped closely together) by tying the boats
at stem and stern, breasted-up, so that they moved forward as one
compact unit.

Most of today's canal traffic consists of single leisure craft with an
average length of about forty or fifty feet, so that there is considerable wastage of water when the lock – consuming some 50,000 gallons
on each operation – is used by a boat on its own. Additionally, a
solitary narrowbeam boat is thrown around a good deal in these
wide locks if the paddles, or sluices, are opened up too rapidly,
allowing a powerful in-rush of water from above. While the more

vulnerable fibreglass or wooden cruisers tend to be controlled with ropes, the stronger steel-hulled narrowboats are generally man-oeuvred on their engines alone, thus saving time and trouble as well as reflecting pride in skilful handling.

Entering, once again, the Braunston bottom lock, we were apprehensive when a smaller hire boat indicated that it wished to join us. Before repainting the boat, we had accepted as inevitable a certain modest degree of knocking and banging between two boats sharing a lock. Now we were exaggeratedly conscious of the pristine condition of *Frederick* and tried to guide in the other boat as though there was a carton of eggs between us. We need not have worried. It transpired in the usual exchange of conversation that occurs when two boats share a lock together that the other boat had been hired by a local chairman of the Inland Waterways Association, an experienced boater and a perfectionist.

At the top of the flight we parted company, as they were stopping for lunch while we had decided to press on first through Braunston tunnel, which, at over 2,000 yards, is the fifth longest in use in Britain. Still not being much experienced in travelling through the longer tunnels and having no great liking for them, I felt that my lunch would digest better after, rather than before, the event.

The cutting soon narrowed sharply into a defile as we approached the ominous black mouth of the tunnel entrance – a small semi-circle, marked by a portico, beneath the hill. For a relatively inexperienced boater, it is a strange and awesome feeling to plunge out of the bright sunshine and open air into a total blackness that is rarely found in westernised society, deeper than the darkest winter night.

Frederick, like other boats, has a headlamp, similar to an old car headlight, and this was angled towards the tunnel's roof. From seventy feet behind, it is difficult to focus on the small glimmer of light that it projects, and we have found that the answer lies in turning on other cabin lights so that the shape and length of the boat is more clearly delineated. Even so, it took several minutes before my eyesight adjusted sufficiently to the utter darkness for me to regain any sense of relative distance and speed, and in the meantime my eyes played all sorts of disturbing tricks.

Braunston in fact turned out to be a more difficult tunnel to steer through than the significantly longer West Hill on the Worcester and Birmingham canal that we had traversed some weeks earlier. The latter is dead straight so that the dim, grey opening at the far end can be identified sooner than in Braunston, where a kink in the middle obscures this encouraging sight. As my eyes adjusted, what I did observe was the yellow pinprick of another approaching boat's headlight, though at this stage it was almost impossible to tell the distance away. The tunnel was wide enough for the two boats to pass, but without too much to spare, so that it was disconcertingly difficult to know when the time had arrived to slow almost to a halt and cling to the near side. One moment it seemed as though the boat was very close, but after dawdling for a while I found that it was still some way off. I increased the speed, taking care not to bang into the Victorian brick-lined walls for fear of dislodging masonry, and then the advancing boat's light was upon us, its cabin slipping past, a brief glimpse of the other steerer in a flash of passing light, a friendly wave and call above the roar and fumes of the two engines, and its stern had passed behind. We relaxed and went ahead.

Now there was a kink to be negotiated, an odd feeling as the headlamp's light seemed to contract the walls like a distorting fairground mirror and the boat miraculously weaved through the narrow section, and, at last, relief on seeing the far end of the tunnel, at first just a slightly less dark point in the blackness, then gradually taking on its half-moon shape and the brightness of daylight. Over the last 100 yards, light started to flush inside the tunnel and *Frederick* broke as though from a chrysalis into sunshine. It had taken about thirty minutes.

The cutting soon opened into expansive meadows, full of grazing sheep, and we pulled in for a quick lunch of freshly baked bread, hot from the oven when bought that morning, English cheeses and summer tomatoes. Then we continued on our way, and soon reached Norton Junction where the Leicester section of the Grand Union turns sharply left towards Nottingham. Months later we were to return from the north this way, but now we continued straight on to the top of Buckby flight.

Here, in Ginger's Stores, we purchased the Anglian Water Authority's licence for the river Nene together with the vital Yale-type key which is needed to release the lock paddle mechanism. Fortunately, we had discovered in advance that this was the only place, apart from the Authority's office in Oundle, which then supplied this essential item.

The small, traditional shop fronting the top lock was the very place where the famous Buckby cans were produced and sold to working boaters; these were the drinking-water containers, highly ornamented with roses, which stood on the cabin roof. Replicas of the style are found in canalside marinas throughout the country and are much bought as holiday souvenirs and gifts. The store was taken over some years ago by Mr and Mrs Ginger, who decided to opt for this life instead of their former executive jobs in Birmingham, and Shirley Ginger continues to paint and sell a variety of Buckby ware.

At the bottom of Buckby flight, after working through another seven locks, we came to a straight mile-long section of canal where three generations of transport development converge and run side-by-side in a living history lesson that spans nearly 200 years. In the middle the canal which dates back to around 1800, part of the great mainline system between London and Birmingham, originally the Grand Junction, afterwards merged to become the Grand Union, once an important commercial route, today a relatively quiet leisure facility. On one side, barely separated by a thin screen of trees, is Britain's first major motorway, the M1, now overwhelmed by the thundering roar of containers and other heavy vehicles. On the other side, an apparently peaceful embankment is frequently sliced by high-speed InterCity expresses, heralded by strident horns, on one of the busiest sections of mainline railway.

As we chugged gently along the comparatively deserted, wide and well-made canal, comfortably transporting our entire home in a seventy-foot boat weighing some thirty tons, we had time to muse over the frenetic rate of modern transport and contemplate twentieth-century advances. Inevitably we pondered on the insoluble problem of whether man's desperate drive for faster and faster methods of communication has brought any genuine improvements in living conditions, when in the course of creating it so much of the natural environment has been destroyed.

Fortunately, this section was soon passed, the canal took a loop away from the motorway and was separated by denser woodland that muffled most of the noise, leaving the motorists to their dangerous pursuits. The railway continued to accompany the canal for most of the next four hours' cruising (and, indeed, railways run close to canal routes over much of the country, not always a disadvantage when easy access is required), although at times the canal swung into quieter backwaters. At Gayton junction we took a sharp left turn away from the railway on to the five-mile arm that links the Grand Union and the river Nene at Northampton.

This descended rapidly through seventeen locks in a sweeping curve down the side of a hill into attractive open country. At the bottom of the flight the canal passed under a massive concrete bridge carrying the ceaseless stream of M1 traffic, and just beyond we could see the Rothersthorpe service station like a frontier post – a welcome stopping-point that I had used many times in the past without realising that the placid canal passed so close to it.

Now we were on a narrowbeam canal with locks only just wide and long enough to accommodate our boat, though of course leaving sufficient clearance at the stern to avoid the projecting cill that marks the base of the previous higher section. At Gayton we had been joined for the weekend by my son Simon, who was making a successful career for himself in London's advertising world, and his girlfriend. With their fresh, energetic help we made fast progress even though the locks were against us because, with another small craft ahead, each one was empty and had to be filled before *Frederick* could enter and be dropped.

In a flight of this type, where the locks are separated only by a few hundred feet of intervening water, it was enormously beneficial to have extra pairs of hands. This enabled us to achieve a steady pattern of work with one of the crew walking ahead to prepare the next lock while the boat itself was in the course of dropping through the previous one. Then, as the boat slipped out of its present lock, another person closed the bottom gate behind it.

With practice, it is still feasible for the two of us to achieve a similar lock-wheeling rhythm, although obviously it calls for greater effort and agility with a good deal of walking backwards and forwards. By-standers often comment on the apparently hard, repetitive work, but fortunately both Lynda and I enjoy these situations, relishing the exercise and finding satisfaction in performing a time-honoured operation skilfully. The old boatmen had many tricks of the trade for speeding the process, some of which are still feasible today, such as shutting the bottom gate with a stern line.

Beyond the last lock of the flight was a new obstacle, a wooden lift bridge, and Simon's weight was particularly useful here. It had to be raised by pulling on a rope dangling from the cantilever arm over the platform. With such bridges there always seems to be a moment when one's entire weight is insufficient to raise it, then suddenly it soars into the air sending the person on the end of the rope crashing to the ground. At this point the beam end has to be held down firmly while the boat crosses beneath.

As the canal passed a few run-down factories and joined the river Nene close to the centre of Northampton, there was little sign of the great expansion of this town that has occurred over the past twenty years, apart from the space-age Carlsberg brewery, a sheer wall of glass facing on to the waterway and offering a bewildering view of myriads of colourful pipes within.

Almost imperceptibly, the canal flowed into the wider river. Being conditioned to the sign language of roads, it seemed strange that there was no sign pointing this way to the river Nene and Peterborough, or announcing the Borough of Northampton. Most of the time on waterways you have to rely on guides and maps to decide your route – there are few signposts.

Under the arches of a stone bridge we reached the first of the locks on the river. This, in fact, was of conventional design, similar to the ones we had just left behind on the Grand Union, broadbeam, and operated with the usual windlass. The first of the special guillotine Nene locks calling for the water authority's key was situated about five miles beyond Northampton.

A minor tragedy occurred here. We had been preceded down the Northampton arm by a small low-powered craft, quite common on the waterways. It was virtually a caravan placed on a pontoon, and propelled by an outboard motor. A charming couple, well into their sixties, were travelling throughout the summer months on it and they had struggled laboriously down the seventeen locks of the flight, making hard work of it. It was only on their arrival in Northampton that they discovered they could not obtain the Nene licence and prized key at this point – they would have to toil all the way up the flight, along the Grand Union, right back to Ginger's Stores.

Since then, Anglian Water has improved the key's availability so that it can now be obtained at Gayton junction; even so, it is still not available in Northampton itself, the point at which most uninformed people would expect to purchase it. At such times you wonder if authorities placed in charge of public rights of navigation wish to encourage leisure use of their waterways.

After we had bade a sad farewell to the confused couple – who had decided to give up the Nene for this year – we passed through Beckett's park. Then the course of the river abruptly turned around the high grassy banks of the new flood protection barrage. The route led through a narrow concrete opening in the wall, with a guillotine gate poised high over it and an official notice stating: 'WARNING. This equipment operates automatically, if the alarm sounds, move clear.' We wondered afterwards about the exact meaning of these words and how quickly the gate descended at times of emergency. Would a seventy-foot boat be sliced in half as the guillotine fell?

Once inside the barrage, the problem took on another, even more sinister aspect. We found ourselves in a vast man-made lake with water stretching within the boundaries of the barrage almost as far as we could see. *Frederick* happily churned along in this enormous expanse of water, as we groped and felt our way along the course of the navigation channel, entirely uncertain about the point at which we would discover an exit, gloomily wondering what would happen if there was a sudden flood surge and we were trapped within this vast dam by the automatic closure of the barrier gates. Would anyone know that we were there? Would we be engulfed in a great tidal wave as water was released into the barrage? Would we be left stranded high and dry as it drained away as unexpectedly as it had arrived?

This is the problem with new developments, constructed since the guidebooks were written and controlled automatically from some unidentified point, perhaps by a computer rather than a person. In the past there would have been a weir under the daily management of a keeper living in his house alongside, aware of passing boats and ready to give advice on current conditions from his immense experience of working there many years. Today, there is a bureaucratic telephone number to call at some distant spot in case of emergency – but there is no telephone box anywhere nearby.

There was, of course, no chance that our worst fears would be confirmed in this driest of summers. But we were relieved to discover the narrow exit on the far side and to come out into the first of the Nene guillotine locks. From this point down to Peterborough there are thirty-three of this type of lock. They were installed during the 1920s so form one of the most recent, extensive series of locks in Britain. At the top there are a conventional pair of mitre gates pointing upstream; these have paddles operated in the normal way with a windlass.

The difference occurs at the bottom of the lock where a solid flat gate of steel hangs on a high gantry. It is raised and lowered by turning a large handle and this is locked in place (to prevent tampering) by the Yale-type key. At our first lock, it took us about ten minutes to discover how to release the locking mechanism, then another ten minutes of cranking to lower the enormous guillotine gate.

The operation, once learned, is not particularly strenuous in itself as the winding mechanism is geared to take the weight. The trouble with the Nene is that it is an absolute rule of the waterway that the gate must be left in the raised position as a safeguard against unexpected sudden flooding, so that, even going upstream, a boater has to go right through the complete cycle of both lowering and raising each gate. It is estimated that each complete cycle on average takes 200 turns of the handle – and that can become quite exhausting over the reaches in which locks occur every mile or so.

With Simon's enthusiastic application we passed through another two locks before reaching Cogenhoe, where the river ambled between meadows full of grazing cattle and horses roaming wild, beneath the square stone tower of the church almost hidden among billowing trees on the hill. We climbed through a field to the charming village street of stone and thatched houses, the first of the sequence of Nene valley villages built from the line of golden stone that crosses England from the Cotswolds.

Simon and his girlfriend left in a taxi to pick up their car from Gayton junction and thence back to work in London. We strolled into the church and learned from the parish guide that the name of this Domesday village is pronounced 'Cooknoe', stemming from the Anglo-Saxon spelling of 'Cocgan-hoh' meaning 'Cocga's hill spur'. Among a mass of other intriguing information, we also found that the Northamptonshire Post Office Directory of 1877 reported that letters would be delivered daily at 8 a.m. and the box in the school wall cleared at 5.20 p.m. Has there been any advance on that?

The sonorous tolling of the bells started to call worshippers to the Sunday evening service. Apparently this is not to everyone's taste, as the Rector refers to the 'hardy annual' of complaints about bell-ringing. It was not always so: in 1909 the then substantial sum of £200 was raised in the village to add three new bells to the existing set, an event that was splendidly celebrated.

As we wandered in the evening shadows through the graveyard, we felt that the bells might help in scaring away Cogenhoe's reputed ghost. Frank Cheer, who lived between 1864 and 1939, was believed to have sighted the apparition in the last quarter of the nineteenth century. According to the parish magazine, he told a local inhabitant that

> he had seen a girl in a long print dress with a basket over her arm coming over the field to the church, and just as he was wondering how she was going to get over the wall she passed straight through it and continued on down to the rectory.
>
> The general opinion was that the young lady had been the daughter of the farmer at Rectory Farm long ago, who used to take that route to deliver butter and eggs to the rectory. She became acquainted with the son of the parsonage, was courted and later jilted by him, whereupon the poor girl is supposed to have put an end to her own life.

It seems that the story retains enough credibility today to encourage gangs of local teenagers to hold ghost-watching sessions at night (or that's their excuse).

In the amber light of the setting sun we descended the hill and returned to *Frederick*, moored on the meadows where the cattle were indolently shifting towards a far corner for the night. On this Sunday evening we were thankful that all our days glided into one another without the disruptive break we used to experience at the end of a weekend on the boat and the exhausting return drive into London. Back on our floating home, the sound of the bells drifted on the soft summer air, comforting and evocative, any harshness mellowed by distance, methodically pealing out the news that English villages survive in the modern world, that traditions are maintained even here so close to one of the new cities of the late twentieth century. Ahead of us tomorrow morning was the start of our real journey down the river Nene some sixty miles and thirty locks to Peterborough and the furthest eastern limit of inland navigation.

Chapter Two

After the drought came the winds

For the first two days after leaving Cogenhoe we travelled downstream fairly fast, in glorious summer weather, for seven hours each day. There was little over the higher reaches of the Nene to distract us and we wanted to press on rapidly to the finer section around Oundle.

The upper river is pitted with minor industrial eyesores. Gravel workings – which around Northampton have been long exhausted, flooded and transformed into pleasant 'leisure pursuit' lakes – seem to be extending further and further to the east, opening dirty holes in the featureless landscape. The river is frequently crossed by rusty iron gantries carrying gravel-loaded belts; at other points low Bailey bridges have been thrown across the water, swaying and dipping under heavy, grinding trucks.

Tentacles of Midlands industrialisation reach out to their furthest eastwards point, extravasating in such small manufacturing towns as Wellingborough and Irthlingborough, where gaunt warehouses and graceless factories encroach upon the waterfront. Elsewhere the river banks are high and overgrown, so not attractive for mooring.

With the approaching August bank holiday, when we expected further visitors, shopping had become a rather pressing need as we had not had access to a good centre for many days. Wellingborough had seemed to offer possibilities but the town looked some distance from the only possible mooring beside a noisy main road.

Eventually, late in the afternoon of the first day, we came upon a smooth grassy bank just before Higham lock, and decided to tie for the night. It was our first stop of the day and we had a late, late lunch at four in the afternoon. The towing-path ran along the bank and local people were sauntering along, enjoying the warm golden day. One brave father had brought his own small children with their nets and jamjars to fish for tiddlers, and on the way he had collected several others from the village.

Finishing our lunch, I glanced up at the bank above the boat. I had not expected to look straight into the large, luminous eyes of a giant bull, ruminatively studying the side of the boat from the peaceful towing-path. He plodded heavily a few steps to peer into the side hatch, open in this warm weather on to the corridor outside the bathroom, while I grabbed my camera and from this position of comparative safety took photographs of the hefty beast, its head hunched on thick shoulders, its distended, powerful equipment swinging between thick hind quarters.

While I was wondering about the bull's potential interest in *Frederick*'s red roof and side panel, two burly policemen, on holiday from Peterborough on a white cruiser tied behind us, climbed on to the bank with their teenage sons and calmly went up to the shaggy animal.

On our journeys around the waterways in *Hanover* we had often encountered bulls. There was a splendid, ancient grandfather in the Lechlade meadows beside the Thames who hardly seemed able to stagger around on his short stocky legs. Then there was a younger, more agile one grazing among his cows at Cropredy on the Oxford canal. But never before, or since, have we been in such close proximity to a substantial bull.

Next morning, shortly after passing through the lock, we had to face another hazard, though this time on the water and man-made: an old medieval stone bridge, no longer used for traffic but retained as a pedestrian crossing. Higham bridge had been placed across the river at such an angle that it was impossible to avoid being carried by the stream directly on to underwater obstructions on the far side. Inevitably, *Frederick* lurched on to the hidden shoal and stuck there. No amount of reversing with the engine and heaving with shafts at bow and stern would shift the boat, firmly wedged some few feet from the bank.

Our seemingly insoluble and miserable situation delighted a couple of young savages from the local tribe who, bored with their fishing, were waiting for just such entertainment. Far from helping us in our predicament, they proceeded to flick water over Lynda until she was soaked, and shouted an amazing range of obscenities. When it looked as though we would have to spend the night on the shoal, a local man appeared on top of the bridge, rounded up the youths and recruited them into helping him pull off the boat with the stern rope flung across to the far bank. Once freed from the trap, I hauled in the rope, put the engine into forward gear and moved away rapidly, waving thanks for his immense assistance.

Time, for once in our leisurely boating life, was becoming a little pressing. My daughter and her boyfriend were expected for the weekend from Plymouth, where Niki was carrying out a three-year Ph.D. research project while Barry was on assignment to the Royal Marines from the Royal Engineers. We had had no chance as yet to stock up for their visit and we had to reach a telephone that evening to arrange a meeting place.

Thrapston was the next sizable town on our route and seemed to offer the right facilities, but again there proved to be no suitable mooring for a full-length boat. Almost before we ourselves had realised, the nearest access point had been passed and this potential stop had to be abandoned. A quick check of the map in approaching the next lock, Islip, confirmed that it would have to be Oundle or nothing; we could at least recall from our previous hire-boating holiday five years earlier that it was an ideal shopping and meeting place, though too far to reach that evening.

We decided to press on through one more lock to Wadenhoe, the furthest point we had reached upstream on our earlier holiday, where we knew there was a lovely mooring close to the village pub, so perhaps also the prospect of a public telephone.

Now we had entered the magnificent section of the Nene where the river roams through wide water meadows, backed on either side by gently rising wooded hills, with limestone villages scattered along its length, always in sight of an elegant church spire silhouetted on the crest. From Titmarsh lock there was an enchanting view across grazing pastures of the square tower of Aldwinckle church like Merton college transplanted from Christ Church meadows in Oxford. Below the lock the river flowed out into an expansive valley, sweeping under a hillside thick with trees, recalling the Thames around Cliveden or Goring, with the spire of the church pinpointing Wadenhoe on the near side, Alchurch's steeple on rising ground opposite.

Beneath a vast, spreading tree on the bank, we found a firm side and deep water to tie for the night. Boy scouts from Thrapston were camping higher among the trees, their green canvas tents set out neatly with military precision, an enticing smell of cooking wafting from the wood fire, while several of them splashed around in canoes and others swung on a rope from a branch over the river. *Frederick* fitted comfortably into its mooring and we walked through the coppice and across a field to the village street of stone and thatched cottages slumbering in the evening sunlight. The Red Lion pub stood at the end of the street, its garden of gnarled apple trees rambling to the riverside.

At the other end of the street, where a stately manor house stood in fine grounds, we found a telephone box. In this peaceful, remote village, unlike so many in ill-treated town centres, the machine had not been vandalised and a call to Plymouth confirmed that we would meet Niki and Barry the next morning by the mill on the outskirts of Oundle.

We rose in good time to reach our destination and found the weather had changed. For the first time in many days it was not searingly clear and bright; we looked out to find the landscape clothed in grey, swirling mist, damp and humid. This was, after all, the first day of the public holiday weekend when, by tradition, the British climate takes a nose-dive.

There were still two locks and five miles to traverse before we reached Oundle. First, Wadenhoe lock itself, followed by a delightful reach where the woods were now on the right-hand side of the river and yet another small village and large church appeared opposite. Then, at Lilford, the river took on an aristocratic appearance as an ornate, balustraded bridge crossed below a substantial country house with deer grazing in its grounds.

The countryside flattened beyond here and the verge of the river spread into reeds as we approached Barnwell upper lock, where the millhouse had been turned into an attractive restaurant. As *Frederick* drew into the lock, well before the appointed time, an extremely sun-tanned, fit and athletic couple in shorts emerged. They looked like hikers on a long open-air holiday. I did not recognise my own daughter as she bounded up; it hardly seemed likely that they could have arrived yet, coming all the way from Plymouth.

'We've been here for an hour, Dad,' she exclaimed. 'We left Plymouth at six, the roads were clear and we came through quickly.'

Shopping had now become of paramount importance as the weekend with two energetic, hungry young people was upon us. We tied the boat below the lock and enjoyed the unaccustomed benefit of riding the mile into town in Barry's car instead of walking as usual – into the long narrow street of stone houses, almost untouched by change, protected by their sheer substance from the noisy passing traffic and the bustle of the congested market around the ancient town hall. It is a place encrusted with history, dominated by the great church whose soaring spire can be seen from miles away, buildings of the famous public school interlaced with shops throughout the centre.

The shops were good and convenient. A weighty turkey, streaky bacon, country-mix stuffing, pounds of local fat sausages, fresh and frozen vegetables, bags of potatoes, Stilton and other cheeses, some puddings and cream, pints of milk, butter, stacks of crusty loaves, bottles of red and white wine, a bottle of Pimms No. 1 and lemonade, together with mint, oranges, apples and lemons. We staggered under the masses of plastic bags and packed them into the car until every corner had been filled.

Barry, already somewhat bleary-eyed from the long drive from Plymouth, wandered around the old streets in a daze, bewildered by the scale of our purchases. Niki looked askance as we heaped them into the car.

'A bit over-doing things, isn't it, Dad?' she queried. 'We're only staying three days, you know, not three weeks.'

Lynda explained. 'We'd hoped to shop coming down-river, but there was no chance to do so.'

'And we are taking advantage of the car to do a bit of stocking-up,' I added. 'Don't forget that normally we have to carry all of this on foot back to the boat. Even so, just wait and see how much is left after the weekend.'

The supplies were loaded on to *Frederick*. Next, we had to replenish the water tanks which had not been topped up since leaving Braunston as, unlike on canals, water points are few and far between on the river. The boat had to be turned into Oundle marina through a narrow gap, perhaps ten feet wide, at a point where the river itself was only a few feet broader than *Frederick*'s length. It seemed almost impossible until we had done it that a seventy-foot boat could be manoeuvred around such a tight corner.

The tanks on *Frederick* hold 450 gallons – a larger amount than most other boats and sufficient to last Lynda and me for at least ten days. With other people on board, it can go much more quickly. The water is pumped from the holding tanks into a header and feeds the kitchen and bathroom taps under pressure, so that visitors perceive no difference from a normal house supply except for the shower over the bath, for which a separate pump has to be switched on to increase the flow. The boat's original owner was a computer engineer and he installed a printed circuit – probably a unique feature – which automatically activates a red light to indicate when the header needs to be replenished.

As we turned out of the marina, even more impossible against the down-stream, and set off back towards Wadenhoe, the morning mist had cleared and the sun produced colours and shadows in the landscape that had been missing earlier.

At a more leisurely pace than our journey down, we returned to Denford where, unusually for the flood-prone Nene, the village street descends to a side channel of the river. Then we went on to Woodford where the church, with its clear chancel windows, is set above a waterside meadow, beyond a long line of tall, serene poplars. There was nearly a disaster on that hot Sunday morning as we walked across the parched fields from Denford to Woodford, and found no sign of a refreshing drink in the old village around the church. It was averted when we discovered a large modern extension to the village on the other side of the hill, where there were three pubs.

The rest of the weekend passed pleasantly in gentle cruising, interspersed with walking and sunbathing, and consuming a great deal of the vast quantities of food and drink we had bought in Oundle.

As Niki and Barry left to return to the West Country, the weather changed again to a pattern that was to remain constant for the rest of our time on the Nene. Although it remained dry and sunny, a strong wind rose that battered the boat persistently and created great difficulties in handling it along the exposed, winding course of the river.

The high, flat surface of the boat with its comparatively shallow draught acted like a sail, so that it often became necessary to counteract this effect in steering from the stern tiller: little problem along wide and straight reaches, but extremely tricky where we had to make a sharp turn around a bend with the stream pushing the stern across. Approaching locks was particularly hazardous since none of them had been built with a sufficiently long entrance channel to afford protection, even though all the locks were capable of taking a boat up to seventy-eight feet in length. We had to adopt the practice of steering right up to the top gates, leaping off and trying to secure lines before the stern was swung over by the wind and stream, frequently with a weir only yards away.

It would have been easier to handle a full-length narrowboat under these conditions on a traditional canal, where normally, though by no means always, there would be a firm bank with bollards for at least a hundred feet on either side of a lock, in addition to virtually stagnant water without the threat of weirs. In these high winds it was strenuous work for two of us to handle such a long boat on the river, not even taking into account the laborious operation of the guillotine gates.

As the tall spire of Oundle church fell away behind us, a new and more elaborate landmark started to take over the skyline: Fothering-hay's octagonal, coronated churchtower, like a miniature edition of Ely cathedral, far across the fens. As the river brought us to the three-arched stone bridge beside the chantry church, the massive tower seemed almost to unbalance the starkly plain chancel with its great clear windows of fine filigree stonework.

Below the bridge, we tied on a meadow where cattle were quietly grazing. Opposite this peaceful spot a mound rose steeply on the other side where a castle once stood. This castle witnessed the first and last days of two ill-starred monarchs: it was here that Richard III was born in 1452 and Mary Queen of Scots tried and executed in 1587.

The wind, as so often happens, dropped in the evening and it became fine and calm. As the sunset gradually deepened into dusk, floodlights were switched on to illuminate the magnificent tower, suspended brilliantly white above the dark trees, and a giant flag flapping from the summit cast weird shadows like ghosts still haunting this place of tragic memories.

While we sat in the bow cockpit, sipping our habitual evening glass of wine, I became aware of closer, more immediate movement in the high, rough bank next to the boat. The ground seemed to be erupting, dry soil spilling away from an emerging bump on the surface. We realised that somewhere inside the bank, not far away, a nocturnal creature was trying to make a new passage from his deep home towards light and air. It continued to burrow, heaving and dislodging soil, until eventually a tiny black pointed nose appeared from beneath the earth, sniffing and sensing our presence. Although we continued to watch until dark had fallen, it never had the courage to come further, but we presumed that it was a mole or one of the small voles that are sometimes seen darting along the water's edge.

The dusk has often been the time when, sitting outside in the bow on a fine evening, we have become intensely aware of the wildlife around us and felt integrally part of it. There was a favourite isolated meadow on the Thames between Oxford and Lechlade which reverberated with distinctive cries of freshwater birds: the rhythmic 'tic-toc' followed by a whiplash crack of the crake and the eerie flute-like 'churr-churr' of the reed warbler, gathering volume and reaching a 'chirruc-chirruc' crescendo.

One night on the Grand Union below Bascote locks, we had been watching cattle go through their evening ritual of gathering as a herd, one or two recalcitrant youngsters skipping away to their own spots, when there was a sudden movement in the undergrowth on the opposite bank, no more than fifty feet away. An animal was moving stealthily around the side of a hummock, an indistinct and colourless shape in the shadow. Then it appeared, silhouetted in full view, a beautiful vixen of rusty tawny colouring, ears sharply pricked as she listened to the night sounds, eyes brilliantly glittering. Agilely, she trotted between the cattle, ignoring their menacing stance, and chased after some prey across the field, weaving patiently through the long grass. Suddenly there was a noisy, careless scuffling on the opposite bank by the hummock and three young cubs skittishly bounced through the undergrowth, less wary than their mother. The bravest frisked towards the cattle, who snorted and pawed the ground, sending the cubs romping towards the safety of the bushes, while the vixen continued to stalk prey across the field until we could see her no longer.

The next day we walked to the top of Fotheringhay's castle mound, now occupied by sheep, and across a bare countryside to the next lock at Warmington. The hedgerows were brimming with deep purple elderberries, so ripe that many were already falling from the bushes; further along, we came across several battered old crab trees decorated with tiny red and green apples. We picked several pounds of both fruit and back on *Frederick* looked up the relevant page of an excellent cookery book that gives recipes for every type of fruit and vegetable; there was one for elderberry and crab apple chutney with no other additives than sugar and spices. The elderberries were easily loosened from their stalks with a fork, but the crab apples, hard and acid, were tough to slice.

The chutney turned out to be superbly tangy and proved to be a perfect complement to Northamptonshire's famous commodity, Stilton cheese. This was our first attempt at using the natural produce of the countryside and now we wonder each autumn why it is that few people seem to pick the fruity sweet elderberry that grows in abundance, far easier to cull than the more popular blackberry.

We continued downstream through three more delightful villages on the way to Peterborough. At Elton a deserted millhouse stood above the lock, and the stone houses were set on a wide grass-edged street with spreading chestnut trees. Then came Wansford-in-England, a limestone village built on either side of the river which seemed to have been lifted bodily from the Cotswolds and transplanted on the eastern side of the country. Perhaps this feeling accounts for the fable that explains its intriguing name.

A seventeenth-century character called Drunken Barnaby is supposed to have collapsed in a stupor on a haycock beside the river, which flooded and carried his resting place downstream. On waking, he discovered with alarm that he was at a strange spot and asked someone, 'Where am I?'

'Wansford,' was the reply.

'Wansford, where?' Barnaby queried.

'Why, Wansford in England,' was the response.

We came to Wansford on a day when early morning sunshine gave a sparkle like frost to the stone houses rising on a hillside above the ancient Norman bridge. Beyond, the Haycock Inn commemorates the tale; then we passed under two further bridges reflecting more recent history. First, the stylish, curved arch of the 1930s Great North Road bridge, proudly carrying the coats of arms of the County of Huntingdon on the north side and the Soke of Peterborough on the south, now merged into the greatly enlarged Cambridgeshire; Then the utilitarian concrete single-span of the dual-carriageway A1. The ancient village of Wansford now lies close to the thundering sound of twentieth-century motorway traffic, an England that would seem totally foreign to Barnaby.

The next village, Water Newton, was also skirted by the unceasing traffic of the A1, roaring north and south, yet on the river there was little sign or sound of it. A long, low farmhouse lay under the shadow of a tall mill and a timeless, tranquil garden sloped to the river's edge where the yellow flowers of waterlilies bobbed on the water. A perfectly proportioned toy-sized neo-Georgian church stood among trees just above the Nene.

There were other bridges on the way to Peterborough. A mile below Water Newton the meadows were crossed by a traditional iron railway bridge which, in many other places, could have been the only survival from a long abandoned line. Yet here it connects with the early Victorian station which is now the terminus of the Nene Valley Railway, one of the great success stories of steam-power revival. The colourful, burnished and restored trains regularly puff and hoot their way along the line close to the river to another terminus on the outskirts of the city.

The entrance to Peterborough by river was marked by an altogether larger bridge which carried the high-speed expresses between King's Cross and Edinburgh, and beyond there seemed to be an endless succession of road, rail and pipe bridges before

Frederick finally emerged under the original stone town bridge into open parkland backed on the far side by the massive line of the Norman cathedral.

There was a firm concrete bank with bollards for mooring along the edge of the park, and another full-length narrowboat (the first we had seen since arriving on the Nene) painted in similar style to *Frederick*, dark blue sides with the name *General Lee* picked out in red and white, was moored there. As I steered towards it we were caught by a sharp gust of wind and turned around, facing back upstream. A man appeared from *General Lee*, gestured for our bow rope, caught it and helped us on to a mooring close by. With a peaked cap at jaunty angle and a broad grin under it, he looked like a young version of Norman Wisdom. A lively, not yet fully grown Alsatian bounded around, trying to help.

Ben introduced himself and Lucy. We were full of admiration at hearing that he had managed to bring his boat down the difficult Nene on his own – apart, that is, from Lucy. A former London docker, he had become redundant when the shipping trade disappeared and had for a time been a lock-keeper at St Katherine's, the Tower of London basin revived for leisure and tourism. Like us, he had decided some six months earlier to spend some money on buying a boat and taking time off away from it all, seeing more of another England. He had found his boat, a converted working narrowboat, at Sawley near Nottingham, and had travelled this far on his own with the ebullient company of Lucy.

It seemed, however, that the situation would change before long. Ben looked radiant as he talked enthusiastically of Cathy, now working as a milkmaid on a farm right by the locks at Long Buckby on the Grand Union canal. After romantically meeting on his way through there they decided to see what a break in the relationship would do, but Ben was aching to return to Long Buckby – and Cathy.

The mooring in Peterborough was ideal, with a lengthy section of firm bank and bollards, a water point and pump-out toilet facilities, and even hot showers in the adjoining public toilet block. All for the nominal charge of £1 per night. In the middle of the park there was a large open-air swimming pool where some enthusiasts were trying to create a summer disco club in the evenings; the music wafted melodiously on the breeze, but it appeared to attract few customers. Between our mooring and the road bridge there was a modern riverside theatre.

This provision of good boating facilities – not always found in towns situated by inland waterways – confirmed our favourable impression on approaching the city. On the outskirts, the land had been attractively apportioned with a fine golf-course on one side and open parkland on the other, containing an expanse of water for sailing and wind-surfing. There was even a sign inviting boats to moor on a side arm of the Nene Park.

Peterborough's roots go back to the Soke, an island surrounded by the tidal fens, on which the Normans built their great monastery dedicated to Saints Peter, Paul and Andrew. In the seventeenth century the innovative Dutch engineers succeeded in reclaiming the land from here to the Wash so that Peterborough is no longer an island, simply a riverside city. In the past twenty years its growth from a relatively small regional centre into one of the towns expanded by planners, using enormous government funds, has been one of the success stories of this policy.

It was about ten minutes' walk from our mooring into the city centre, where a vast two-tier shopping mall has been constructed behind the original frontages, providing excellent services without spoiling the traditional market square, one side formed by the fortress-like gates to the quiet cathedral close.

We walked through the doors of the immense west front and into the ethereal atmosphere of the Norman building. This was completely open and uncluttered from end to end, giving a feeling of light and air, while the lines of stout pillars on either side of the nave provided an impression of strength. Hanging from the marvellous painted ceiling was a dramatic red and gold cross suspended over the sparkling gold and silver marble reredos of the altar – the only interruption in the long through view. The choir was singing evensong and filling every remote corner of the great building with their sound.

Peterborough's excellent mooring and facilities gave us a very good base for a few days' break from travelling while we sorted out our affairs. First, we went to the post-office to see if there was any mail addressed under the *poste-restante* system. Many post offices throughout the country will accept personally addressed mail and hold it in pigeon-holes for collection. When we rented out our house

and left London, our friends John and Penny had nobly and kindly
agreed to allow their flat to be used as a forwarding address for our
mail. As they were both keen on the inland waterways, John having
his own sixty-foot narrowboat *Shalford*, they had been to visit us
often over the initial months, bringing the post with them, and we
had also collected it from them on fairly frequent visits to London.
However, there had been a gap in these two-way visits over the
preceding weeks so that, for the first time, we had asked them to
use the *poste-restante* system.

There was no sign of the fairly substantial package that we knew
had been despatched at our first call at Peterborough post office.
Two days later, I returned. Still no mail. The next day was to be
our final day before leaving so I returned then. When I was told,
once again, that there was nothing for David Bolton, I suddenly
realised that I had not asked for Lynda Rolfe, and sure enough
there in the box marked 'R' was the package addressed to 'David
Bolton and Lynda Rolfe'.

It so happened that none of this was necessary in the end since
Lynda had to make an unexpected business visit to London.
Peterborough, again, proved to be the ideal centre with the station
fifteen minutes' walk across town from the boat and a fast, regular
InterCity service. Even so, it was on these occasions when unscheduled meetings were called in London for either of us from time to
time that the conflict between one way of life and another was
heightened. Inevitably, business meetings created an intrusion into
our relatively placid way of life, as we had to gear ourselves up
mentally and dress up physically, and both of us became nervous
and irritable before and after these events. While we recognised that
we were fortunate in one way to continue earning some money, we
often felt that the continuation of our working links, which we had
not expected originally, caused an intrusion out of all proportion
into our sabbatical year.

Ben, accompanied by Lucy, set off back up-river on the day Lynda
went to London, and when she returned to *Frederick* we started to
prepare for our own departure.

From our mooring in the park there were another four miles of
wide, straight river, terminating at the Dog-in-a-Doublet lock; after
this the river, though navigable, flowed into the tidal, treacherous

expanse of the Wash – not a safe place for a narrowboat primarily designed for calmer waters. The crossing to King's Lynn and from there into the Great Ouse has been made by some narrowboats with advice from experienced pilots who know the tides and shifting sandbanks, and it is made more frequently by locally based cruisers better shaped to cope with the potentially rough conditions. This year, we did not have the time to tackle this route into the East Anglian waterways if we were to reach our intended winter base at Lapworth, although I hoped to return another time and travel by boat to Cambridge, where I had grown up and first acquired a feeling for water when rowing on the Cam for my college eight.

It was extremely galling to see another channel almost opposite our mooring which led from the Nene into King's Dyke, connecting through the Middle Level navigations with the Great Ouse and Cam, but it passed through Stanground lock, which cannot take boats of over fifty feet in length, although the beam can be up to ten feet. On our original hire-boat holiday, five years earlier, we had started from the drainage sluice below Stanground and passed through this deep lock which forms part of the flood-control system of the fens; now this was impossible.

The distance separating the Nene from the Great Ouse at Salters Lode lock is about thirty miles, and there are a variety of access routes which are designed for drainage purposes and used for the shipping of local agricultural products. While both the Nene and the Ouse are capable of taking boats up to seventy feet in length – the standard throughout the Midlands canals – this connecting system between Stanground and Salters Lode prevents a natural interchange of boating between East Anglia and the rest of the country. Development of tourism along the Great Ouse, one of England's finest rivers, leading to Ely and Cambridge, is stultified by this one short bottleneck.

One source of the problem lies in a bureaucratic anomaly. Anglia Water Authority is responsible for navigation on both the Nene and the Ouse (as well as other waterways in eastern England). King's Dyke, built as a drainage channel, comes under the authority of the Middle Level Commissioners who have little interest in navigation (and, in fairness, have responsibility for flood control in a difficult area).

Fenland District Council a year or so ago made a thorough and balanced study of the situation, concluding that navigation formed an important part of this water-based leisure facility, and there are plans to improve the immediate environment with better paths and signs. Yet no one so far seems to have taken up the real issue, which is that the existing navigation could be upgraded so that it could take boats of a length regarded as standard throughout the rest of Britain.

This is only one of several similar problems which we were to discover on a journey through England where different waterways come under a variety of authorities, none with any over-riding interest in or responsibility for improving links between one section and another. Next to Stanground, the most notable issue is the proposed Avon link with the Grand Union canal at Warwick. Here, the river is wide and deep enough to carry locally based boats over separate reaches which have weirs maintaining a satisfactory water level between Warwick and Stratford, but the absence of locks means that there is no through traffic.

A proposal put forward several years ago by the Higher Avon Navigation Trust showed that it would be relatively easy to open this ten-mile stretch of the Avon, thus for the first time providing a through route for wide-beam craft from the Thames to the Severn. The plan was abandoned in the face of local opposition, but has been re-examined more recently with some hope of a successful outcome. We were to hear much more about this situation when we reached the Avon the following year.

Returning upstream in persistently forceful winds, we overtook *General Lee* in a quiet corner on the edge of Oundle. Ben had found the going difficult against the stream and the high winds. He had stopped to lay in a big stock of wood for the Aga which was always alight, heating water and cooking, an acrid pungent smell of wood smoke trailing behind the boat.

At Oundle, once again making the almost impossible turn into the marina to top up our water tanks, we met with another lone navigator, though in a very much smaller boat. Keith Eley was patching a hole in the side of the fibreglass canoe in which he had transported his camping equipment all the way from Wolverhampton, where he was the BWB keeper for the flight of twenty-one locks.

'That's a long way to have paddled,' I exclaimed. 'How far are you going?'

'To Great Yarmouth,' Keith replied in his nonchalant manner, as though it was just around the next bend.

'Great Yarmouth!' I quickly assessed the geography and realised it was on the far east Suffolk coast. 'What, all the way by water?'

He pointed to a small wheeled trolley. 'Yes, all the way by water, except for the odd place here and there when I push it over land.'

'It's really possible?'

'Well, I don't know yet because I have to find out. But, yes, I think so. And I hope to succeed because I'm doing it for charity sponsorship. In fact, this will be a shorter journey than last year, when I covered the round route from Wolverhampton up the Lancaster canal and back, 162 miles in all.'

Tall, slight and wiry, Keith Eley returned to examining the repair in his canoe. 'I think that's going to be firm in a few minutes. I must press on because I'm a bit behind schedule – I'm supposed to be meeting friends at Yarmouth in a week to go sailing in an old Norfolk wherry.' He paused to look into the distance. 'Then, next year, what I hope to do is canoe from the Midlands to the Thames and right along the old Thames–Severn canal link – it would be a fascinating trip.'

It seems that there is no limit to the adventurous spirit that the waterways bring out in different people. Wishing him well, we departed in the opposite direction, feeling somewhat humble about the style in which we were seeing the country.

Two locks further on, we again caught up with *General Lee*, seemingly moored in midstream, a mouth-watering smell of cooking mingling with the wood smoke. It looked as though Ben had stopped and was preparing his evening meal.

'An odd place to have moored for the night,' I remarked to Lynda as we approached.

Ben emerged from the cabin and shouted above the noise of our engine, 'I've gone aground on shallows. I kept on trying to get off but only became more deeply embedded, so I thought I might as well settle for the night. Now you've come, I'd be glad if you can try and pull me off.'

Lynda steered *Frederick* cautiously past a sandbank that seemed to spread across most of the river. Ben threw his bow rope which I tied to a stern dolly. Revving both engines, we started to pull *General Lee* away, but it was a long process as the hefty weight behind *Frederick* tended to swing its bow off direction. As we gradually succeeded, we appreciated *Frederick*'s dual assets of powerful 46 h.p. engine and relatively shallow draught. Like most converted working boats, *General Lee* sat much deeper in the water and, since that experience on the Nene, we have often found that *Frederick* can pass through silted canals which cause endless problems to older boats, originally designed to carry heavy loads at a time when frequent traffic kept the waterways better dredged.

'You did that like one of the old working girls!' Ben shouted to Lynda joyfully as his boat was cleared of the shoal.

We joined forces for the rest of the journey back along the Nene. *General Lee* and *Frederick*, in their similar livery, looked like father and son and attracted a good deal of attention on a river where the sight of even one full-length narrowboat is rare. It was enjoyable to have the company and good to share the effort of working through the upper half of the river's locks.

A day or two later, a month after we had arrived on the Nene, we parted ways – Ben heading back to Long Buckby and his milkmaid; we turning south towards Aylesbury, Lynda's home town. Ahead of us was England's longest tunnel, Blisworth. Behind, the Nene's thirty-eight guillotine locks which we had passed through twice; this meant that, with the extra bank holiday excursion, we had wound the handle of the lower gate mechanism through 16,000 revolutions. It had become a boring, tiresome operation and we relished the prospect of being back on the more straightforward, traditional locks of the Grand Union, yet taking with us many memories of a lovely, quiet and much underused river where we had at least avoided the drought problems of the Midlands canals.

Chapter Three

Along the Grand Union

We had timed our return to the Grand Union to coincide with the reopening of Blisworth tunnel, which at one and three-quarter miles is the longest navigable tunnel on the English waterways. It had been closed for nearly four years for major reconstruction of the middle section at the time we turned at Gayton junction down on to the Nene, and had been reopened with much rejoicing and a grand ceremony as we returned up the Nene.

The years during which Blisworth had been shut had caused intense frustration to boaters, effectively cutting off the southern waterways from the Midlands and northern ones. It left the Oxford as the only through route and that canal – narrowbeam and heavily silted in parts, with recurring problems of water shortage and already over-used at peak periods – was not suited to take much additional traffic, particularly the older traditional boats.

There had been gloomy predictions when Blisworth closed late in 1980 (and at that time it had been open for only a short while after an earlier long closure) that it would never be reopened: it was thought by some that the tunnel had reached the end of its troublesome life.

We reached Bletchley on the Grand Union at the end of our first summer of weekend cruising on *Hanover*, intending to continue the following spring through Blisworth to Braunston. During the winter BWB had been noncommittal about Blisworth's future; then, in March 1981, BWB announced that the tunnel would be closed for two or three years while the middle section was rebuilt. They provided a facility for lifting boats overland from one end of the tunnel to the other; we thought about using it, but decided to take the alternative waterways route to Braunston by tracking back along the Grand Union to Brentford, up the tidal Thames to Teddington, and thence along the river to Oxford.

The BWB plan to transport boats overland from Blisworth was an ironic twist of history. When the line of the original Grand Junction canal was completed in 1800, from Brentford to Braunston (linking with the Oxford canal and the Midlands), a gap remained in the ridge of hills separating the Nene and Great Ouse valleys between Stoke Bruerne and Blisworth. Little progress had, for all sorts of reasons, been made on the tunnel started four years earlier, and in the meantime the gap was bridged by constructing a railway over the hill between the two termini. Boats had to be unloaded at either end on to horse-drawn wagons.

Blisworth's history has been fraught with the problems caused by the difficult terrain of clay, rock, limestone and ironstone which shifted, particularly in wet weather, causing distortions to the tunnel lining. From the start in 1793 of building the Grand Junction, the engineers realised that a tunnel would be needed and that it would be a major problem. Work on the original concept was begun a year later with a completion date set for June 1797. Difficulties were compounded when the original contractor resigned, work continued on a small scale under direct company supervision but ground to a halt as the costs escalated and uncontrollable quantities of water seeped into the workings.

John Rennie, a leading canal surveyor, and Robert Whitworth won a competitive tender in 1796 for a new alignment of the tunnel, but work still proceeded so slowly under these appalling conditions that it was gradually abandoned in favour of the urgently needed over-the-hill tramway which came into operation in August 1800.

A year later, rapidly increasing traffic on the canal resulted in an unacceptable and costly bottleneck, forcing the Grand Junction company to think again. William Jessop produced plans for a tunnel which would be sixteen and a half feet wide with a total height from the crown of the arch to the bottom of the waterway of eighteen feet, with the side walls two bricks thick. It was estimated that 600,000 bricks would have to be made (and it was found that the clay soil was ideal for this purpose); the prime difficulty of seeping water was to be eased by cutting drainage sluices.

The renewed effort to build Blisworth tunnel started in late 1802. It was finished successfully in early 1805 but not before there had been many traumas and fracas between the penny-pinching company and its contractors, and some loss of life among the workmen. The method finally chosen for building the tunnel provided the solution.

People, naturally, think of a tunnel being bored from either end and meeting in the middle. Blisworth – to deal with the problem of ground movement and water seepage – was constructed by digging out shafts from above and down to the level of the tunnel, then working outwards from each one.

The first step was to mark out a straight line over the hill and this called for a sighting point which was provided by the tower of St Mary's church at Stoke Bruerne, so that the tunnel was exactly lined towards it. Then a longitudinal survey gave the rises and falls of the terrain over the level of the projected tunnel. The position and depth of each shaft was calculated from this combined information.

Starting from each end simultaneously, a total of nineteen pits were dug out of the surface down to the depth of the tunnel and the soil was pulled out on horse-drawn lifts, creating mounds of earth that have survived. Most of the shafts were filled in after completion, though four were retained to provide ventilation, brick-lined and built like chimneys above the ground to create a draught that has become more necessary since the introduction of diesel engines.

The result of this brilliant engineering solution to an apparently intractable problem was the construction of a tunnel which is dead straight – unlike Braunston and King's Norton – so that today's boater can see from end to end on a clear day. Even so, the unsound geological strata have caused the tunnel to be dogged with a record of repair closures throughout its history.

We passed through Blisworth only two weeks after the latest reopening and felt rather more confident about its condition than others we had experienced previously. The original brick lining remained at either end and a lot of water was seeping through here, but a precast concrete tube had been inserted into the middle section, slightly increasing the width. It looked strong and solid, and naturally all boaters hoped that it would provide a lasting solution to the latest problem.

The weather had been overcast when we entered the deep cutting at Blisworth leading to the tunnel entrance, but we emerged into brilliant sunshine at the far end – what a difference one and three-quarter miles can make to the British climate!

Stoke Bruerne – a charming village of houses, pub, restaurant and shop fronting either side of the canal – has become one of the best known places on the English waterways since in 1963 a disused grain mill was turned into the National Waterways Museum. The atmosphere of boating people at the heyday of the canals is conveyed by life-like exhibits particularly a realistic replica of a boatman's cabin and a family group wearing traditional clothing and we were delighted to see a photograph of a rather younger Ron Hough painting roses and castles.

The building of Blisworth tunnel is well documented, and the exhibition includes Jessop's own engineering drawings and diagrams together with pages of financial costings. Elsewhere in the museum are displays of the primitive tools used by navvies in digging out the tunnel and cut, fascinating photographs of many well-known working boats and their crew, and records of tolls levied on individual craft, now much sought after by their current owners who have restored and converted them.

The early Victorian canal age brought about a greater need for systems of controls and authority than had previously been required for commercial transport, and the museum has many examples of disciplinary signs – some cast-iron, some painted on wood – to control weight over bridges, impose charges, prevent fishing and swimming and set standards for boat decoration. An alternative aspect of society is seen in many newspaper advertisements and posters whereby offenders 'apologised' publicly for breaking the rules, presumably a nineteenth century equivalent to the public ridicule of the village stocks.

*

From Stoke Bruerne, the Grand Union meandered like a river through open agricultural country until becoming hemmed in by dense housing and factories at Wolverton, one of the small group of semi-rural, semi-industrial towns tied together as a conglomerate by the planners of the twentieth-century city of Milton Keynes.

From the road, the planners' dream of a new garden city had bewildered me – it seemed to consist of a complex network of peripheral roads identified by such strange symbols as MK2 and MK3. The scene from the waterways proved to be more rewarding. After Wolverton the four distinctive sails of a windmill, dramatically placed on a hillside at New Bradwell, beckoned, and the canal passed on to a plateau. Below, there was a lake with great flocks of birds rising and falling above the water, and we could hear the distant sounds of their harsh cries. It was open country, with hardly a sign of buildings.

We came around a bend and passed a secluded church, set in parkland on the edge of the canal at Great Linford, where the traditional village had been carefully retained.

From here, towards the southern perimeter of Milton Keynes, areas of new building and industry came closer to the waterway, but the building work had been planned to take advantage of the environment: here, an open park, there, detached houses and flats set around a marina, elsewhere, landscaped lawns and shrubs separating the canal from denser housing and schools – and the occasional perfect Victorian villa had been preserved. Along the length of the canal, firm new paths weaved among thickets and grass.

There had clearly been a genuine effort within Milton Keynes – better than anything we had seen before, or since – to create an attractive environment around the canal, yet there was a strange feeling that most of the people seemed to be so sad, rarely giving the friendly call and wave experienced elsewhere, particularly the fishermen who glowered into the water, never exchanging a greeting.

The lock-free pound from Cosgrove ended at Fenny Stratford's stop-lock, we passed through a swing bridge between porridge-coloured brick cottages and entered one of the most glorious parts of the Grand Union. This took us through a valley of soft hills, up a flight of three locks at Soulbury – where the canalside pub was a gongoozler's delight – and twisted past sandy high banks to come into Leighton Buzzard. Then we crossed the fertile agricultural plain below the striking ridge of Dunstable Downs, ascending through several fine bridges and locks.

At Marsworth we turned off the mainline at the foot of the flight carrying it, past three reservoirs to the summit at Tring, and then dropped through a staircase lock on to the narrowbeam arm leading to Aylesbury, where Lynda had grown up. After the Grand Union broadbeam locks, which we had shared with two other boats over the last stage, it seemed like a toy canal, though a very pretty one, with bridges so generously curved that they almost encircled the waterway. The square tower of Marsworth church, standing on a hill, rose step by step behind us as we dropped on to the flat plain, backed by the sharp green Chiltern hillsides. It was a day of clear sunshine, though a cold wind caused some difficulty in steering in and out of locks.

A grey high-rise concrete block with jagged edges, totally out of character with its surroundings, pinpointed low-lying Aylesbury and, dropping through two more locks past unassuming Victorian and Edwardian terraces, we arrived in the small basin in the centre of the town. It seemed to be bursting at the seams with narrowboats and dwarfed by an ultra-modern glass-fronted office building, yet there was a time when the basin's survival – and with it the Aylesbury arm – had been threatened with further encroachment.

The Aylesbury Canal Society has maintained a firm policy of welcoming short-term visiting boaters, non-members, and *Frederick* was fitted into a comfortable berth, jostling happily among other craft. The Society turned out to be a lively and enthusiastic bunch of people – a few residential, but mostly leisure-time, boaters – who provided excellent club-house facilities and well supported social events over the year. Many of them have explored out from their home base to the furthest extremities of the English waterways and they have an annual competition to see which member has covered the greatest distance.

We were made to feel very much at home in Aylesbury, where Lynda's mother lives, and she came on board the boat with some of her friends. On the return up the arm to Marsworth we were joined by Lynda's brother Douglas and his young son Gareth, who discovered that he could manage to open the mitre gates and entered into the spirit of lock-wheeling so enthusiastically that we were sure he must grow up into a boater.

As we turned back on to the mainline at Marsworth, our thoughts of the winter were becoming more pressing. We were aiming to return to Lapworth before maintenance stoppages closed many routes.

Boaters planning to winter afloat can be differentiated from summer swallows by the growing pile of firewood on the cabin roof. On our way through Milton Keynes I had noticed the quantity of jetsam floating in the cut; in Aylesbury I purchased one of the wire rakes with upturned ends which are used to weed lawns, and returning through Milton Keynes we had a competition to see who could collect the greatest amount of driftwood by fishing with the rake. It proved to be fairly ineffective, but it gave us some fun.

The main stocking-up of the winter fuel was achieved at Buckby wharf between the top of the Buckby flight and Norton junction, where an arm led to Leicester and the Trent. Although the township of Long Buckby, two miles away, was bordered by a conflux of modern transport – the M1 and A5 in parallel, the Northampton BR line cutting away from the Euston–Birmingham mainline – it remained serenely unaffected by these developments within sight and sound. As though on an island out of the main stream, the inhabitants have carried on their own way of life at their own pace, a sprawling community where everyone knows everyone else and all their family history, a microcosm of traditional English rural life.

The coal merchants, Collins, were down a side street leading from the tiny square of shops. Over a discursive chat in the kitchen with young mothers surrounded by babies and pets, a delivery to *Frederick* was arranged. The lorry arrived in the afternoon, driven along the canalside track by one of the wives, who, we were told, often dons a leather jerkin and heaves the sacks herself. On this occasion the job was done by her husband, who loaded about three-quarters of a ton through the deck hatch into the bow compartment.

The bottled gas supply for cooking and the refrigerator was on an equally large scale for a boat: two 47 kg propane containers housed in a steel locker with external access and venting. Each cylinder lasted for nearly three months, but this large size was not readily available from boatyards. Again, at Long Buckby, there was no problem and another local firm was happy to deliver straight on to the boat.

John Groves, a local marine engineer, came on board to sort out in his usual unassuming, practical way one or two minor mechanical and electrical faults that had developed. His working visits have always been enlivened by the latest Long Buckby gossip, especially about his part-time service with the local fire brigade (often called out to deal with horrendous motorway pile-ups), together with accounts of salmon fishing in Devon and pheasant shooting in Yorkshire. He is a true countryman.

Tied round the corner on the Leicester arm we found *General Lee*, and Ben – looking radiantly happy that Cathy had decided to give up working as a milkmaid and join him on the boat. We adjourned to the pub by the top lock where she was working in the evenings, and she served us with scampi and chips. She was young and attractive, glowing with outdoor healthiness and affectionate warmth.

We set out again through Braunston tunnel, negotiating its awkward kink in the middle, dropping down the beautiful flight – a deep valley with sheep pastures and farms on either side – past the Admiral Nelson where in summer customers sit outside with their pints. Below the bottom lock, where months earlier we had completed the repainting of *Frederick* in the covered dry dock, we tied among pairs of traditional narrowboats, sheeted over, dark smoke curling from black, brass-bound chimneys above the boatman's stern cabin – a timeless scene.

Climbing a steep path from the middle bridge through fields to the village street, we bought freshly baked bread at Goodness Foods (run by an evangelical community) and fresh meat from Pete the Meat, and wandered into the church standing on the edge of the hill, its serated spire a welcome landmark for boats approaching from the north and west.

The verger broke off from polishing the lectern to talk proudly about the church that, he felt, belonged more to the community than to the succession of rectors – who have to be Welsh – appointed by Jesus College, Oxford. He apologised for the fact that the church, the third on its site, was only 150 years old and took us to the font, the only remaining remnant of the original Norman foundation, where a replica Buckby can stood ready for christenings.

'Have you seen our knight-in-armour?' he asked as he directed us to a corner where lay an almost perfect effigy.

'He was a de Ros – d'ye see the rosette emblem between his feet? We think that he was passing through Braunston on his way back from the Crusades when he died, since his feet are turned inwards and his sword sheathed.' The verger patted him affectionately. 'Poor chap, he'd done his fighting in the Holy Land and then finished here, no one knows how or why.'

The outer surfaces of his shield and upper body were noticeably more polished and worn than the chainmail. 'Aye, he's had to suffer that indignity too, when farm workers sharpened their scythes on him – there's no stone from around here hard enough for sharpening.'

'So, you come from a boat? 'Course, Braunston isn't what it used t'be in those days,' our companion continued. 'D'ye know that Cross Street, where's all council houses now, was a lovely line of old cottages where the boatees – that's what we called them and no disrespect meant – lived between their boating? In them days, before all this council housing and decline in canals, Braunston used to have three butchers and thirteen pubs.' (I thought, with two butchers and five pubs it was still better than many other comparable villages.)

He pointed out that Braunston had always been at the crossroads of transport over the centuries. 'Watling Street just over there and Fosse Way on t'other side – the Romans brought us prosperity. Then, traffic on the roads from London increased and all those travellers used to have to stop at the foot of Old Road at one inn or t'other. After that, it was humming when the canal came, boats unloading on the old wharf; and then we 'ad the railways, they crisscrossed every ways around here. Braunston was a great stop for them.'

He paused and looked around the church reflectively. 'Now, it's all changed – them motorways and InterCity lines, I suppose they're all right in some ways, but it's by-passed us and it leaves a place like this stagnating. We used to be a centre of transport, but no longer.'

He talked in such a way, expressing strong personal feelings, that it seemed that he himself had experienced the entire process of change from the Romans to the present day. The centuries evaporated as he conveyed an impression of the heavy tramp of the Roman legions, the faltering horse of a dying Crusader, the thundering hoofs and rolling wheels of stage-coaches drawing into an overnight stop, the wild shouts and cries of horse-drawn narrowboats on their exhausting route between London and Birmingham, and the heavy puffing and shrill hoots of steam trains. Generations of his ancestors, without break, must have lived in this place, never moving away, observing the change going on around them, and our friend had inherited this ethos, and could feel it pulsating within his blood. To him, it was not history, it was Braunston which had remained the place where his predecessors had lived, their home, around which external developments had taken place, leaving the community of Braunston with an amalgam of unbroken, collective memories.

Chapter Four

Christmas at Lapworth

We passed over the aqueduct between Leamington Spa and Warwick that carries the Grand Union on three well proportioned stone arches some fifty feet over the river Avon only hours before it was scheduled to be closed for more than four months. Extensive repairs to prevent leaking had to be carried out on one side.

Peering over the stone balustrade, we could glimpse the river, quite deep and wide between tree-lined banks, a tantalising reminder of those hot summer days back in Stratford. Now we had entered a small section of the waterways completely isolated from the rest by a ring of winter maintenance stoppages; we had emigrated, in effect, to the Midlands for four months and banished ourselves from the south. Moreover, neither of us had any real experience of living in the country in the winter.

Our patch of water was circumscribed by other lengthy stoppages on the north Stratford canal and, at the Knowle flight, the south Stratford would be virtually impassable (as in most winters) as the National Trust grappled once more with the never ending task of repair. Our boating, effectively, would be limited until late March to the long pound between the Hatton and Knowle flights.

In past years, when the canals were still heavily used for commercial transport, stoppages for repairs and maintenance occurred unpredictably as and when necessary. This could have meant unexpected delays of several days or even weeks, leaving no choice for the pairs of working boats but to tie up in an ever-lengthening queue, unless there was a place to wind the boats and take an alternative route. The work, of course, was carried out as quickly as possible as such delays caused severe hardship to the crews, most of whom depended on payment when the heavy loads were delivered. There were no closed seasons in the days when freight had to be kept on the move.

Nowadays the system has gradually changed to meet the conditions on most waterways today: little or no commercial traffic and a leisure season lasting from March through to the end of October. British Waterways Board has adopted a policy of concentrating maintenance work between November and March, apart from those places where more serious problems, like Blisworth tunnel and Anderton lift, have caused prolonged closures for perhaps two or three years. Following the publication in late October of the winter stoppage programme, there will be many different points throughout the system where locks, tunnels and bridges are shut for periods ranging from a few weeks to a few months.

This policy favours hire-boat operators by keeping most of the waterways open throughout the months of heaviest demand. Sadly, it has severely restricted any extensive cruising in the winter and it curtails freedom of movement during months which to many enthusiasts offer a different experience and quality of boating. In fairness, though, BWB generally arranges the schedules so that there is a break in the programme over the Christmas and New Year period when all but the longest closures are lifted, and there is a marked trend for more and more people, including some hire-boaters, to taste the delights of this holiday season.

There was to be no such respite, however, in the extensive repair work on the Warwick aqueduct, which was to be closed until late March. As we passed over, only hours before the section was due to be drained, there was a feeling of unreality, knowing that we could not return south this way for four months. Being adjusted by now to an attitude of mind that thought primarily in terms of waterways, it was little compensation to know that we could travel south by road or rail.

Just beyond the aqueduct we ascended the two locks at Cape of Good Hope on the edge of Warwick and stopped to take on water. The tap was placed in such a position that *Frederick*'s stern fitted snugly into the curved side above the top gates and, being broad-beam locks, there was ample room for another boat to pass out. Even so, some fifteen minutes later a hire boat came out and rammed into our stern.

Lynda ran back to see if there was any damage and remonstrated with the steerer.

'You're lucky we were so competent or it could have been worse,' came the reply.

'But we've stopped to take on water,' explained Lynda.

The response was, 'Why do you have to take on water *there*? It is very selfish of you to block the passage of other boats!'

We were almost ready to depart and start the ascent of Hatton's twenty-one-lock flight, but decided that we had no wish to do so in such company and stayed on for an early lunch, hoping that the other boat would have gone far ahead.

Hatton is not the longest flight in England; the record is claimed by Tardebigge where thirty locks meander gently uphill on the Worcester and Birmingham canal. Hatton ranks equal second with the Wolverhampton flight, but there is no dispute that it is the most impressive and awe-inspiring since many of the twenty-one wide-beam locks can be seen from a point close to the bottom ascending the hill in a straight line like giant black-and-white steps.

The first time we had tackled Hatton, some two years earlier in *Hanover*, it had seemed quite daunting and there was a point about halfway up the flight where we looked back at the locks already accomplished, and upwards at the layer upon layer of locks still to come, and wondered if we would ever reach the top. Since that time we have come to enjoy working through the flight which, once conquered, provides a great sense of achievement. We have worked it in the company of other boats (on one occasion breasted-up, tied together like a pair of old working boats), which of course shares the physical exertion, but reduces the pleasure since other crews always seem to want to set a record-breaking time.

On our own, we can achieve a steady pace and rhythm in lock-wheeling which is satisfying and rewarding on a flight of this kind where the locks are spaced relatively close together. The slower rate of progress allows one time to look around and absorb the near surroundings and expanding view, as the hill ascends, of spacious Warwickshire countryside, back to St Michael's tower soaring above the historic city.

Over a long flight we switch tasks at every third or fifth lock so that the work is shared equally and on cold windy days it has often been a relief to hand over the steering. Lynda has complained bitterly on occasions when I have 'stolen' one of her locks!

This November day we were fortunate in having mild, cloudy weather, with a rare burst of sunshine – perfect conditions for the job. All the locks were against us since the previous boat had already passed out of sight and there was no boat descending. It meant that we had to go through the complete cycle of first emptying each lock and then filling it again, so I reckoned that three hours and twenty minutes to the top was a good time for two people handling a full-length boat.

We had a little help on the way. A friendly retired keeper closed the gates for us at the bottom lock, amidst some cheerful chat about the old days. Then, halfway up, the resident lockkeeper, Peter Ballard, looking exceptionally smart in a peaked cap, broke off from trimming the hedges to give us the same service. When we reached the last three locks (which emerged from behind a bend just when we thought we had beaten the flight) Mr Ballard had cycled up and prepared them ready for us.

He remarked on how quiet the day had been with only six boats up the flight, none down it. 'In the summer, I would have fifty boats through here in a day,' he said. Like a Cornish shopkeeper in the off-peak season, he seemed to be glad to have the time now to enjoy the slower pace and the chance to talk with customers.

Still smarting from our unfortunate experience at the Cape, I remarked cynically about the competence of hirers.

'Most hirers are pretty good and careful,' he replied. 'Many come year after year, often in the same boat. Those that don't know much about locks before they arrive at Hatton have learned all about them by the time they've passed through.'

He advised us, with the late afternoon daylight fast fading, to tie in the cutting above the top lock, among a small group of other boats. The next morning we continued on the long pound, first passing through the short Shrewley tunnel and stopping again on the far side. Here there was a smaller dark, dank passage leading sharply up to the village, built so that the horse drawing the working boats could be walked up and over the hill while the boats were legged through the tunnel.

There was a telephone box in the village street at the top. Every Friday we made it a practice, if possible, to contact our London offices to check on whether there had been any urgent messages or correspondence during the week. By now we had become adjusted to a way of life in which for us there was no rigid five-day working week, no sharp division between weekdays and weekends, so it seemed slightly strange to talk to our ex-colleagues and hear that they were in the process of clearing their desks of work at the end of the week. To us, now approaching our winter base, it seemed that an entirely new period in time was starting.

The three or four miles from Shrewley to Kingswood formed one of the most attractive sections along the entire length of the Grand Union. The canal meandered like a river, following the gentle curves of hillsides, and crossed a high embankment at Rowington from where there were splendid views of a countryside epitomising the English scene, sadly ploughed under and destroyed in other parts. Here there was still an enchanting patchwork of small green fields of different shapes and sizes, enclosed by hedges and trees to give shelter to the cattle and sheep grazing on the pastures, the rolling landscape dotted with warm redbrick and black and white buildings.

Two elegant feathery larches on a wide sweep of the canal, followed by a high roving bridge. Kingswood junction. We turned sharply left into the side arm. After 500 yards a narrowbeam lock lifted *Frederick* into Lapworth basin, where the north and south Stratford canals met. We had reached our adopted home base for the winter months.

A small white house stood on the spit of land separating the top lock of the south Stratford canal from the basin, and the entrance was crossed by a perfect, miniature cast-iron footbridge, its two sides cantilevered to provide a tiny gap in the middle designed originally to allow unimpeded passage of the rope of horse-drawn boats. These bridges are a charming, distinctive feature of the canal.

Old brick buildings – the National Trust's maintenance base – formed a yard around the other side of the lock and along this side of the basin was a coppice of firs, a favourite picnic spot containing tables and barbecue grids. Beyond, the bottom lock brought the north Stratford canal – starting some thirty miles away at King's Norton on Birmingham's outskirts – into the basin.

A splashing waterfall cascaded over a side weir next to the lock, while the far edge of the basin was silted, merging into tall willowy reeds, among them the gaunt skeletons of long-deserted wooden craft, driven into the mud as their last resting-place.

We had discovered Lapworth back in the early summer when we were looking for a suitable place to start the mammoth external repainting of *Frederick*. At Kingswood junction the canal was deep enough to tie immediately alongside a firm concrete bank, making it an ideal place to work. There was another full-length narrowboat in similar dark blue, red and white colours, though it was marked out as a conversion from an old working boat by its riveted hull, large wooden rudder and magnificent arched tiller, ornately painted and decorated with traditional woven ropework.

On that day in high summer there had been a lively, animated group of people around the boat: a mother, perhaps in her thirties, dressed attractively in a flowing dirndl dress, bouncing a happy, plump child on her knees; an older bearded man in blue overalls who looked as though he had just finished work, a pigtail tied beneath a squat blue cap crushed on to his head. They were joking and laughing with a couple from a pair of traditional Braunston camping boats tied further along. Frisking among them was a slender black dog.

Snatches of conversation reached us. 'Dan, behave or I'll tan your hide.' 'Blisworth, good grief, d'ye remember the time we were passing through and collided with another boat?' 'Eric, he's only tired and needs a rest.' 'Yes, they were across the middle and didn't know what happened. Ruthie, I love you both!!!'

Lynda strolled past them, catching more fragments of conversation. She reported: 'The man seems a bit rough, but the woman has an amazing upper-class accent.'

The next day, we met Eric and Ruth Hunt, young Dan (then not two years old) and their sixteen-year-old dog Sasha. We learned of their differing backgrounds. Ruth's perfectly cultivated, modulated voice had been acquired at a well known South of England boarding school, though her home was in Yorkshire; she had trained first as an opera singer, and then as a nurse. Eric, after starting life in Hammersmith and then working on a Buckinghamshire farm, had adopted the Midlands some twenty years earlier as the appropriate home for a skilled engineering draughtsman. For the past sixteen years he had lived on *Sandalwood*, a converted BCN butty, at Lapworth, bringing up on his own a previous family of one son and two daughters. Ruth had joined him some four years ago, they married and Dan arrived on the scene. Sasha had been around for many years.

As the initial tentative contact started to grow into the first roots of a friendship that was to deepen and expand in the future, we found Eric and Ruth to be the warmest and most natural people that we had met so far on our travels. It was clear to us, so newly arrived on the scene, that they had a deep interest in and loyalty to the waterways, and an appreciation and understanding of the environment that went far beyond our own experience at that time. Although Ruth's background had been well endowed and Eric's brother had made a personal fortune, they were totally content with a way of life that was simple and satisfying in its own right. That is, if you could accept Eric's acerbic humour.

One summer's day we had taken a coffee break from painting the boat when Eric asked: 'What are your plans for the winter? If it's a severe one, you're going to need somewhere where you can count on a water supply. You could think of coming here – we've never failed to have running water, even in the coldest of winters. You may even find that you like our company!'

We were delighted and flattered by the suggestion, which came at a time when nagging doubts were starting to arise about the way in which we would cope with our first winter afloat.

'It's a great idea, Eric, and we'd certainly love to think about it,' responded Lynda.

'Lapworth would make a superb base for the boat,' I added, 'but can you guarantee the behaviour of the neighbours?'

Keeping in touch by letter on our journey down the Nene to Aylesbury, we had developed and confirmed the plan to return to Lapworth for the winter, despite the restrictions on movement that subsequently emerged from BWB's winter closure programme. Our contact with the Hunts had inevitably been spasmodic, so that we were a shade apprehensive on arriving back at Lapworth, now that we had committed ourselves to this cut-off canal island, and we were not certain what Eric and Ruth really felt about our return.

We found *Sandalwood* not on its own mooring in the first pound of the south Stratford, where Eric and Ruth had cleared and cultivated a glorious summer garden of flowers and fruit trees, but in the basin itself, and the Hunts emerged to give us an ecstatic welcome. Any lingering doubts about our choice of winter base (and company as the days shortened and the weather hardened) were banished in the warmth of the reunion. Eric's news, however, was less reassuring: maintenance work on the Stratford canal meant that *Sandalwood* had had to be moved into the basin, possibly for the duration of the winter, and there was also rumour of work on the north Stratford affecting conditions in the basin itself.

Eric introduced us to Stan Turner, who had been lockkeeper at Lapworth for the past sixteen years and was much respected by boaters. He saw no reason why we should not tie in the basin to be close to the water point when the weather turned colder. For the present, however, we preferred to stay on the mainline by Kingswood Junction, in a more open situation with pleasing views up and down the Grand Union and, opposite, a meadow attracting a variety of water birds.

About five minutes' walk along the towing-path from the junction was the bridge for a minor road between Hatton and Hockley Heath, a link between the main Stratford and Warwick roads to Birmingham, some twenty miles away. Next to the bridge, with a garden on to the canal, was the Navigation Inn – flagstoned, with low beams and great logs burning in the snug fireplace – a genuine local patronised both by the village folk and the commuting business people who had moved there.

A scattering of retail outlets along the road provided for a rather mixed selection of needs: a garage, a garden centre, a ladies' hairdressing salon, an off-licence, a car distributor who also sold bottled gas, and a general stores with a daily supply of delicious fresh bread. Under the railway bridge and up the hill, there was a second cluster of shops including a butcher, electrician and the sub-post office which provided a dry-cleaning collection service, with another pub just beyond.

This community, strictly, was called Kingswood and consisted for the most part of fairly modern detached houses around the railway station. Lapworth itself was a small village of old houses, mostly converted into luxurious commuter dwellings, surrounding the ancient church on a twisting side road some two miles away. The railway station, about half a mile from the canal, provided an hourly service between Birmingham and Leamington Spa, with connections to Oxford and Paddington, and to Stratford by changing at Hatton. It had been a further reason for selecting Lapworth as a winter base when, at that stage, we had planned to sell the car.

We changed our minds around the time that we were leaving the river Nene and starting to plan more positively for the coming winter. Little use had been made of the car during the summer, and it became an embarrassment when we left it for three weeks in a Stratford street, the police traced its ownership and called on our tenant to trace our whereabouts. Yet, somehow, the right opportunity to dispose of it never arrived.

One day, I said to Lynda, 'How do you feel about keeping the car, now that we've come so far, until the spring?'

'I'd been thinking the same thing,' she replied. 'As we've no real experience of a winter afloat, it could be a great asset, especially if we became ice-bound for weeks – we could use it to collect supplies, even water.'

'I agree. I think that it's the one luxury we deserve. Although we haven't missed it at all so far – in fact, quite the contrary – when it comes to wintering it will be a nice change to get around, see and do other things away from the boat.'

So it had been decided. The car had been left some two months earlier in the safe-keeping of the very helpful garage by Long Buckby station.

Just after arriving in Lapworth, I set out one morning to walk to the railway station, catch the train to Leamington and change on to the Paddington line. After dealing with some business in London and checking with the tenant on the state of the Islington house, I returned the following evening from Euston on the round trip back to Long Buckby, the station in a cornfield. As it would be long after their closing time, I had warned the garage of my plan and there was no problem. As arranged, the car was standing in the forecourt with the spare keys hidden inside it, a new MOT certificate and invoice on the front seat. I put a cheque in the letter-box and drove away. This ready trust and helpful co-operation from such people – whom I had not known until a few months before nor seen since – has been one of the most heart-warming features of travelling around the country.

I left the car in the park next to the picnic site under a clump of fire trees and for some time we made little use of it. First, we wanted to explore the immediate vicinity on foot since it appeared from the Ordnance Survey map that there should be paths fanning out in every direction. Stage by stage, we discovered and developed a variety of walks starting from and finishing at the boat.

A walk made almost daily by one or other or both of us was to Potterton's sub-post office. Instead of going up the road we could follow the towing-path past the first two locks of the north Stratford canal, under the first road bridge and turning off by the second. The all-important telephone box providing our vital link to the outside world was situated right there. Often we continued up the rest of this lovely flight of fourteen miniature narrowbeam locks, each with its own small pound and each set at a different angle in the gently rising hillside, surrounded by a model countryside, penny-sized fields enclosed by little clumps of evergreens: a modest, warm, and friendly landscape compared with the open expanses of East Anglia we had left behind.

One section of the flight, where leisure craft permanently moored, had been drained already and a triangular gantry placed over the lock to lift out the old gates and fit new ones. The boats were resting uncomfortably on the oozing mud bottom and there is no sadder or more ungainly sight than a boat out of water.

Going in the opposite direction down the south Stratford canal, we came across boats in the same plight in the de-watered second pound. Beyond, the tree-lined canal continued through a soft valley of sheep pastures edged by woods. At Dick's Lane stood a typical feature of this waterway, a barrel-roofed single-storey white-washed cottage which could have been transplanted from a Greek island. From here there was a choice between a short cut to the Grand Union or a much longer walk to Lowsonford, a pretty hamlet, with another option of returning across water-logged fields to Rowington and back along the mainline.

A bridle path through the wood parallel with the Stratford canal, one field away, took us to a number of walks in a deep secluded valley, and eventually we found that from here we could climb to Lapworth church, returning back down the north Stratford canal. We were horrified to learn that the rural peace of this remote countryside, at present reached only by narrow lanes, was threatened by the M40 extension.

There were two National Trust properties which could be reached on foot to the north: Packwood House with its immaculate clipped yew hedges said to represent the Sermon on the Mount, and Baddesley Clinton, an impressive fortified Tudor house. From the latter, there was a walk along an avenue of beeches to an isolated church, and beyond to the only extant reminder of the once great Forest of Arden immortalised in Shakespeare's comedies. A still more distant variation of this walk brought us back to Tom o' the Woods pub at Turners Green on the Grand Union.

On fine days and free days, there was a sufficient variety of walks ranging in duration from less than one hour to about three hours to give us exercise, fresh air and a widening understanding of the changes in nature which continued, almost imperceptibly, throughout the winter. In the country, we found that there was no abrupt divide between the seasons: autumn, winter and spring elided into each other in a gradual process in which silver satin buds, sharp pointed green shoots and fluffy catkins had emerged before the last dried brown leaves had fallen. It seemed that the moist warmth of these Warwickshire valleys represented the furthest tentacle of West Country flora: here, the bridle-path banks were thick with moss, ivy and ground cover which encouraged early flowering violets, whereas only a few miles east into Northamptonshire the landscape took on a different, more barren character.

While the November and December weather remained relatively benign, we travelled in *Frederick* as much as possible along the one open section of canal. First, we went to the northwards limit of navigation to Knowle, where the flight of five locks ascended dramatically on an angle cut into the curve of the hillside. From a pleasant mooring at the bottom, we walked into the prosperous market town which had become our most accessible shopping centre.

We returned back along the Grand Union as far as we could go to the top of Hatton flight, and turned in the splendid winding-hole that had been created for the ceremonial opening in 1934 by the then Duke of Kent of the up-graded section of canal. In 1929 the Grand Union Canal Company had been created through the merger of several independent companies, and the government contributed £1 million to building fifty-one new broadbeam locks, replacing narrowbeam ones, between Braunston and Birmingham in the last major attempt to restore the declining traffic. The object had been to provide a route suitable for sixty-six-ton wide boats, but this was never achieved as the scheme ended before conversion of the last flight of narrowbeam locks into the centre of Birmingham. Today's boater has benefited by having use of one of the best built and equipped sections of canal in the country.

All this time, *Sandalwood* had stayed tied up in the Lapworth basin. We had hoped that they would join us on these excursions. 'Are you coming to Knowle today, Eric?' had become a regular joke between us. Then, late one afternoon, Eric, who liked to move on when the mood took him, started the old Armstrong-Siddeley engine and plodded down the arm to join us by the junction. What his engine lacked in propulsion compared with the Mercedes was compensated in its evocative, soft, steady chug-chug-chugging sound.

Eric has a remarkable talent with mechanical objects and, as a trained engineer, he cannot bear to see anything discarded before the end of its useful life. The engine in his boat, originally an unpowered butty, was a prime example of this genius; it had lain, rusty and abandoned, in deep meadow grass for many years. He took it apart, piece by piece, cleaned and scraped each item, replaced parts where necessary, refurbished, reassembled, tested and installed it on the boat. This fine example of past British engineering skills, now perhaps forty years old, had been restored to provide the main drive and power of the boat, twice its age.

The internal layout of *Sandalwood* was entirely different from that of *Frederick*, apart from the engine room, packed with Eric's ingenious mechanical surprises, at the stern. Entry was through hatches on either side of the hull, about halfway along the length,

with two steps down and the certainty on the first visit of banging
your head. From here to the bows was the kitchen and main living
area, with a solid fuel fire, the sides deeply lined with bookshelves,
the walls filled with pictures and items collected over the years,
cluttered compared with *Frederick*, yet expressing the comfortable
feeling of a place much lived in and loved. In the other direction,
towards the stern, a series of compact cabins led off the narrow
corridor, each retaining some connections with Eric's now grown-
up family, though one had recently been converted to accommodate
Dan's cot.

Sandalwood tied next to *Frederick* on the mainline, so that when
Eric and Ruth came on board after putting Dan to bed they could
hear whether he cried out. It was the first of many similar evenings
during the winter as the days shortened and the nights lengthened
when there was time to sit on one or other of the boats, in the
warmth of the fire and the muted lighting of paraffin lamps, a glass
of wine in hand, mulling over our contrasting experiences of the
waterways.

To us, so newly converted to this way of life, these sessions were
like teach-ins. Eric had been fortunate in coming to the canals a
couple of decades earlier when there was still the opportunity of
helping on some of the last few working craft. We had picked up an
assorted jumble of impressions over recent months, gossip and
hearsay about past conditions, which he helped to clarify and put
into perspective. He had known what it was like to work a pair of
narrowboats from Gas Street in the centre of Birmingham, the
crossroads of Midlands canals, learning from the old boatmen their
techniques for speeding the process: partially lifting a top paddle to
swing shut the bottom gates, gently urging open a gate with a
pushing prow, pulling shut a gate with a slip-knot line from the
stern. Practices officially frowned on today, yet unavoidable when
one man could have been handling a pair of boats on his own.

Ruth delved into filing cabinets to produce albums bursting with
photographs of their past travels to Braunston, Northampton and
Leighton Buzzard, pictures of working boats and their crews, while
Eric gave a running commentary about the history and style of each
boat, where it had been built and for what purpose, who had bought
and converted it subsequently. At other times, Eric would sit quietly
in a corner with a hemp of new rope and in thirty or sixty minutes

of absorbed painstaking work twist it into the intricate interlaced patterns – a string or a Turk's head – that have traditionally adorned the boatman's cabin or tiller.

There were stories of Lapworth's murky past, when a few years back it was alive with itinerate boats forming something of a commune, its members enjoying a free and easy lifestyle. There was the sad account of *Daisy Ashford*, which caught fire on a day when Eric knew there was a dog alone on board. Ignoring the danger, he crawled under the pall of acrid burning smoke to rescue it. 'Then the ungrateful beggar bit my hand,' he said.

As the wine glasses glinted in the warm light of the lamps and the atmosphere became more intimate, the conversation drifted, broadening, into families, life and literature. Modestly, almost apologetically, slim volumes of poetry were unearthed which we took away to read quietly on our own. One of Eric's poems struck a particular chord:

> I don't want to be trapped in an office again
> Imprisoned by concrete and glass,
> Pretending an interest that doesn't exist
> And wearing a flat on my arse.
> Bored by a colleague telling me how
> He narrowly missed violent death
> At the hands of some idiot driving to work
> Leaving him quite out of breath.
> I must break the chain of green pound notes
> That threaten the rest of my life,
> Stand on a hill
> And shout
> I'm alive,
> I'm free and I'm sane,
> Though I'm broke!

Although the long, dark, winter nights encouraged these joys of companionship, they were a problem in other ways. On *Frederick*, we were dependent on 12/24 volt lighting drawn from the pair of domestic batteries, and this was too faint to enable certain types of work to be done after dark; it was frustrating that we had the time but not the conditions. Moreover, the pumps used to circulate the central heating as well as operate the bath shower and waste were a heavy drain on this same source.

Early on, we were careless about using electricity and – ignoring a rapidly diminishing picture on the black and white television screen – succeeded in exhausting the batteries completely. Fortunately, Eric was on hand to save the situation. Among his treasure trove in *Sandalwood*'s engine room, he had a restored generator and voltage control board. Tying the two boats alongside each other, stern to stern, extension lines were run across to *Frederick* and a powerful charge put back into the batteries. We were much more conscious, after this accident, of the need to conserve our resources as well as maintain the batteries, so we made a practice of running the engine for at least two hours each evening when the heaviest demand was put on domestic services.

Outside the comfortable confines of the cabin, the winter nights were a revelation: rarely, and only when the sky was overcast, was it as totally dark as the interior of a tunnel. Many nights, a faint slither of moon gave sufficient luminescence from the water to walk around, using a torch here and there to clarify a dark patch, probe into a gloomy shadow. A fuller moon brought nights so clear that often a torch was unnecessary, the surroundings standing out in a strange, ghostly silver light, each separate object starkly silhouetted – flat, lacking depth, like stage scenery. Sometimes, after a day of overcast cloud and misty rain, the sky cleared and the landscape became illuminated, surrealistically, in brilliant white light.

On such a night of pure silver light, when the frost in the air created sharp fluorescent sparkles on the trees and grass, I went to make the regular evening check on the water level and boat's moorings, and the thin, icy air carried the ethereal sound of voices:

> Hark the herald angels sing,
> Glory to the newborn King,
> Joyful all ye nations rise,
> Join the triumph in the skies.

A carolling choir was travelling through the village on a float decorated with multi-coloured fairy lights, and they warmed the chill night air with their melody. Christmas was upon us, and suddenly we realised just how much there was to do.

We went to an exhibition of paintings at the home of local artist Trevor Boult and immediately fell in love with his drawings and pictures which captured the essence of inland waterways. On a one-stop shopping expedition, I solved the perennial problem of Christmas-present-buying for the family – that year, everyone had a Trevor Boult picture.

We took one of our favourite walks to a little wood erupting with mole hills beside Lapworth church, picked bunches of holly bright with red berries and returned to decorate *Frederick*'s cabin. We drove into Knowle, a place that boasts four butchers compared with only one supermarket, and collected an enormous fresh turkey, returning in the dusk past the gardens of large houses where the trees were illuminated by coloured fairy lights, at one point strung in a dancing line across a pool of water.

Two days before Christmas, Niki arrived from Plymouth, shortly afterwards joined by Simon from London; the turkey was stuffed with chestnuts, banked by plump sausages and slowly cooked in the oven; we put on the assorted funny hats that Niki had bought in Knowle and exploded party poppers; an amazing selection of presents were broken from their tinselly wrappings; we played charades and acted out book and film titles. We were holding our first Christmas afloat.

It was fortunate that we had celebrated the event one day early. As Simon and Niki returned to the south, I felt the first tremors of a pain that made it uncomfortable to sit down. By Christmas Day, when we went on board *Sandalwood* to exchange presents, I was feeling sufficiently ill to refuse Ruth's invitation for Christmas lunch, and by Boxing Day morning it was obvious that I could not undertake the drive to Aylesbury to join Lynda's family celebrations.

When Ruth called round to check on my condition, she found me wrapped in a duvet, packed with comforting hot-water bottles, and she urged us to contact the local medical practice. From the telephone by the post office we reached the duty doctor, who gave sound advice on hot salt-bath treatment. We followed his prescription.

The surgery was due to open the next day after the holiday break, but before I could set out, the virulent boil that had caused so much pain had broken. A day later I went for a complete check-up and received reassuring news. 'It was just a nasty boil, like any other boil, but you're very fit and the body has dealt with it in the normal way.'

Two days later, John and Penny came from London for New Year's Eve. Penny arrived looking exhausted by the drive and drawn by a severe cold which she was trying to contain. Despite her valiant efforts, she had to retire to bed for the evening, while by now I was feeling fully recovered, fit and ready for the celebration with Ruth and Eric that we had missed earlier. We crossed over to *Sandalwood*, carrying the traditional piece of coal, together with a bottle of whisky, and drank a midnight toast to Penny's rapid recovery. As the chimes rang in the new year, Lynda and I wondered about the experiences that it would bring, especially over the rest of the winter.

Chapter Five

When the snow and ice came

New Year's Day, as so often seems to happen in England, arrived deceptively warm and sunny, and the canal towing-paths around the Lapworth basin attracted a constant stream of noisy, happy families, trying to walk off the excesses of the holiday season before the imminent return to work and normal conditions.

The benign weather was not to last. Just as we were wondering if we would be granted an exceptionally mild winter, the first ice formed across the basin. In the evening, the water was ruffled by a light breeze. The next morning I looked out across a flat, smooth, glistening film of ice, almost totally covering the expanse, and realised how quickly conditions can change.

Eric was around early with the news that Stan Turner had told him that BWB intended to drain the basin the next day to work on the bottom lock of the north Stratford canal: it would be wise to move both boats into the arm below the connecting lock, where the water level would be maintained as part of the long pound terminating at the Hatton flight.

Frederick was still on its Christmas mooring below the high brick wall alongside the first split bridge over the south Stratford canal. *Sandalwood* was tied on the side of the basin next to the coppice of fir trees. We started to prepare for the departure. Although the ice was thin and we had to move only some 300 yards, it turned out to be a difficult operation, taking more than an hour of hard work. Being the nearest to the lock, we started to move *Frederick* first, immediately finding that broken wedges of ice packed between the bow and the floe, throwing the boat off course and making it impossible to steer. Ruth and Lynda took shafts to smash the sheet of ice in the lock entrance while I gradually manoeuvred the boat backwards and forwards.

Stage by stage, patiently, *Frederick* was negotiated into the lock. Now, in lowering the level, we had to be careful that fragments of ice did not wedge around the hull, perhaps dangerously suspending the boat from the lock sides. Below the lock in the narrow channel the ice had formed more thickly, so that a passage had once again to be cleared by breaking it with shafts from the bow before, finally, *Frederick* was eased into the mooring on the far side.

Sandalwood followed behind, using the clear passage, and tied immediately below the lock with the sidehatch facing on to the towing-path, thus giving easier access for Dan and Sasha. The two narrowboats were opposite each other, separated by the width of the canal, and to reach the other side we had to cross a narrow plank over the bottom gates.

It was fortunate that we had moved when we did. By the next day the basin was drained, leaving only a small stream of water from the weir flowing across the muddy bottom. Apart from the obvious discomfort of living in a boat that was sitting awkwardly and at an angle, we would have lost the moderating protection of water around the hull, especially vital to the internal pipes placed below water level.

The ice that had started as a thin skin hardened each day in bitterly cold weather, until before long it formed a thick crust across the canal. In the narrow gap between the hull and the bank, the ice started to push against the boat so that it became a regular morning duty, wearing a ski anorak and gloves, to smash the ice between the bank and the boat from stem to stern. One day conditions were so arctic that even this energetic exercise could not keep me warm, and

I had to break off halfway along and go back inside the boat to thaw out by the fire. Eric said the temperature had dropped to minus 12 degrees centigrade overnight.

Further along the arm, living alone on a cruiser beyond the railway bridge, Margaret White had an even tougher job. She had to keep the ice broken all the way around the craft to prevent it from being compressed and lifted above the water – the structure of a fibreglass hull needs the support of water to hold it rigid. Valiantly she stumped around the frozen canal, keeping a few inches clear around *Sundowner II*.

One morning her anguished screams of protest made us aware of another threat to her safety. A steel narrowboat that had been moored temporarily for a few weeks in the arm had started to move, which involved the laborious process of smashing a passage ahead. As it approached *Sundowner*, Margaret realised there was considerable risk that a razor-sharp slice of ice could be pushed against the hull, piercing it like an arrow. She prevailed on the crew to ensure that the ice around her mooring was crushed to smithereens and, under her threatening eyes, they battered with a shaft from the bow, pulverising the surface.

In former days, the regular passage of heavily loaded boats kept the canals clear in relatively cold temperatures and when conditions became severe, ice-breakers were used to reopen routes. These were short, slim boats with a reinforced pointed prow, originally pulled by teams of horses. A beam ran down the length of the boat at shoulder height and gangs of men stood on either side, swinging rhythmically like bell-ringers to rock the boat and smash the ice. For an old boatman locked immovably at a remote spot in solid ice, it must have been an exciting sound to hear the ice-breaker approaching from far away: horses tramping and snorting, men shouting and singing, the ice splintering.

Enthusiasts have converted a few of the surviving ice-breakers into cruising craft, easily recognisable by their distinctive elegant lines. Sadly, there are no longer any ice-breakers used to keep open the canals in the winter.

With the ice strong enough to walk on, there was inevitably talk of the potential hazard of falling through it. The lockkeeper told me that there had been some five cases of people drowning in this way in recent memory. There had been a young woman who had disappeared after being seen to walk down the bottom lock of the north Stratford flight, where the path under the road bridge was steep and extremely slippery. Her body was found after the thaw and it was believed that she must have skidded and slipped right under the ice.

What happens if you are unlucky enough to fall through the ice was a topic of discussion one evening in the Navi. During a previous hard winter one of the customers had been talking about this. 'Hold your breath and look upwards for the dark circle,' he was advised. 'The solid ice appears to be lighter than the place where it has been broken.' On his way back from the pub, he staggered over the frozen canal while taking a short-cut, fell in and lived to return and confirm the correctness of the advice.

I did not try to put the theory to the test, but there were many nights when we returned late to *Frederick*, crossing the treacherous narrow plank on the bottom lock gates with great caution.

Sasha was the only one to have a terrifying experience. Late one evening, after having a meal on board *Frederick*, Eric went out to check on Dan, who was sleeping on *Sandalwood*, and Sasha followed him. Before anyone realised what had happened she had slipped off the plank into freezing water on the edge of the ice. There was no time for deliberation. Eric seized a hank of rope, twisted it into a noose and, seconds later, lassoed the animal by her neck and jerked her back on land. Retrieved, she collapsed unconscious for a few minutes, but in the warmth of the cabin soon revived, shook herself and looked around.

The ice created problems for the wildlife around us. The ducks, at first, skidded and slipped in all directions, their webbed feet splaying awkwardly on this unaccustomed surface. Gradually, they too learned to cope with it and some became quite skilful at sliding and skating over the ice. They seemed to enjoy the sensation. The mallards took turns at swimming round and round in circles to keep open a pool, so that they had water to drink and safety from the nightly threat of predators.

One morning Eric said, 'Come and look at this.' From the lock, we could see a distinct line of pawmarks on a light covering of snow over the ice. The trail led towards the open pool in the basin, where there was a flurry of disturbed snow. 'Looks as though there was a fox prowling last night,' he said. Even so, it seemed that its hunt had not been successful as there were no scattered feathers or other signs of a kill. We hoped that the pool had given safety to the ducks.

Eric, after so many winters in Lapworth, identified some of the ducks by name. There were Captain, Duchess and Bluebeak. They slithered across the ice between the boats, desperate for food, and the most brazen jumped on to the side deck, knocking on the cabin wall. Unlike park ducks, who are used to being fed with stale bread, these gobbled any surplus food, snapping up cheese rind, bacon fat and vegetables.

We had particular concern for a maimed Canada goose, a sad-looking solitary bird that had been left behind after the exodus of the flock from the field opposite our mainline mooring. Its long neck seemed swollen and distorted, and it was able to eat only a little food at a time. It looked as though some object had become lodged in its throat, and Margaret told us that she had once plunged her hand and arm right down the neck of a goose in a similar condition, bringing up the offending item. In this case, the bird survived without such drastic action and eventually improved.

An elegant black and white pied wagtail often came tripping and dipping on the ice outside the boat, while on the branches of nearby trees we hung string bags of nuts that attracted a variety of brilliantly coloured tits, swinging acrobatically.

There were less welcome visitors, like a scavenging rat that we had to chase away. We were not prepared to take any risks since we had heard horrifying stories of the way in which these vermin can quickly establish themselves and breed in the bilges. Margaret threatened to shoot the animal on sight with the pistol she kept for self-defence (and she had formerly taken part in competitive shooting). We were always expecting to hear the sharp crack ring out across the night air, but I believe it was a threat never executed.

Soon after the ice formed, the first flurries of snow fell; before long, the world about us had become almost completely covered under a white sheet. There was a coating of hard snow on the canal's frozen surface, on the roofs of the boats and over the surrounding countryside, even though the initial falls were of light, powdery snow, barely deep enough to cover our shoes.

A modest thaw followed and the Hunts decided to take advantage of it to drive to Yorkshire and visit Ruth's family, since her father was retiring as senior partner of a solicitor's practice and her mother was giving up the chairmanship of the local magistrates.

We took responsibility for *Sandalwood* – ready to light a fire and heat the boat if the freeze returned – and their black cat Twpi, a nomadic wanderer who appeared from whence we never discovered as regular as clockwork for his evening meal placed outside the boat. Despite our blandishments – even on bitterly cold nights – he rejected our invitations to enjoy the warmth of *Frederick*'s cabin.

I discovered that playing understudy to Eric was a demanding role. When he was there, he spent a good deal of time ensuring that our living conditions were maintained trouble-free. A fresh water supply was the most important service, and I recalled his remark back in the summer that he had never been without drinking water over sixteen years at Lapworth. This called for checking, first thing in the morning and last thing at night, that the water tap in the nearby boatyard remained turned on to a small trickle so that the minute flow of water prevented the pipe from freezing. We had to insure against the well-meaning but ill-informed actions of passers-by. The secret was to sustain this tiny flow of water.

Although the tap was some 300 yards away, we were able to connect the supply with the boats by means of an almost endless series of hose-pipes that Eric had acquired over his years of boating. He also ensured that we maintained a good level of water in our holding tanks by topping them up fairly frequently, just in case the supply was aborted. After filling the tanks on each boat, every section of pipe had to be separated and drained carefully to prevent any chance of water freezing within the tubes.

The Hunts had been away for four days when we awoke one morning to see a black sky, overcast with clouds burdened with heavy snow. Soon, a blizzard obliterated everything outside, isolating us in the warm cocoon of *Frederick* like an igloo from a moving wall of great soft snowflakes. During a brief respite in the afternoon, I stepped outside into a deep drift and looked back to see the boat encased in cotton wool snow. I ploughed through the snow to check on road conditions.

That evening we were due to go into Leamington Spa to see a production of *The Importance of Being Earnest* at the Loft Theatre, the splendid home of an amateur dramatic company that has earned a reputation for its professional standards. We were keen to see it since a friend was playing the role of Lady Bracknell. Traffic had kept the road open, so we decided to risk the ten-mile journey, even though the sky looked forbidding.

It started to snow again, lightly, on the way into Leamington, but on reaching the town we found that the broad streets had not been salted or cleared, so conditions were more hazardous than in the country. But it proved to be worth the risks of the journey, Anne giving a magnificent performance, the play sparkling with wit in every line. In particular, I was able to confirm my hazy recollection that Algernon – when he deserts London society to peregrinate in the country – talks of going to 'Bunbury'. I knew there was a place of this name on the Shropshire Union which we hoped to reach in the spring, and I began to wonder whether 'Bunburying' had any connection with our own roving way of life.

Although further snow had fallen while we were inside the theatre, the road was clear enough to return to Lapworth. The next morning, I lit the fire on *Sandalwood* as I was certain the Hunts would be returning that day. They were back before dark; the motorways had been open but the last few miles through Warwickshire countryside had been difficult.

It was just as well they returned when they did. Over the next three days the snow continued to fall, at times as a blizzard driven by a fierce bitter wind, at other times dropping more gently in immensely large flakes. It snowed and snowed until it seemed that it would never cease. It piled in great drifts outside the boat so that we had to clear a path before stepping out; time after time, we had to sweep a way through the snow to reach the lock, cross it and continue to the water point or the car parked in the spinney. Cautiously, step by careful step, we were able to make our way along the towing-path, past two locks, and reach Potterton's stores to buy essential supplies and make telephone calls from the box.

The local road, which must have been rated as a low priority for snow clearance, looked virtually impassable. When, three days later, I had to drive from Lapworth to Warwick I found that a snow plough had been through at some stage, clearing a single one-way passage through drifts much higher than the car's roof. On this particular morning, however, the police had cordoned and closed off the road from Warwick to Banbury, and announced that there was no route open to the south.

Although ice and snow persisted in Lapworth – and the local

roads remained restricted by deep drifts – our life was never seriously interrupted. Friends and business colleagues made one-day visits from London to see how we were faring and went away greatly impressed by the warmth inside the boat and the beauty of the all-white countryside, the snow retaining an Alpine-pure brilliant whiteness, unsullied by dirty traffic and pollution. We were full of admiration for the people who undertook long journeys in these tricky circumstances, although more than once we spent an anxious hour or two waiting in the Navi for them to arrive.

In February, Niki came from Plymouth for a long weekend as she was playing for the South of England Reserves in an all-Britain lacrosse tournament at a Birmingham sportsfield. It seemed, at first, unlikely that it would take place, but there was a brief respite in the weather on Saturday, the tournament was begun and lacrosse-players would not be deterred from finishing the competition once started. Through swirling snow, we saw players (some red-legged in shorts) flailing wildly with their lacrosse sticks and racing around the pitch. Niki emerged, from her favourite back position, out of the snowstorm, driving on her team with desperate invectives; they must have had the right effect since we later witnessed her receiving the silver trophy for the winning team in a pavilion steaming with exhausted bodies and hot cups of Bovril.

The following weekend Rosemary and Simon drove over from their lovely weekend cottage at Cropredy beside the Oxford canal to join us at a Royal Shakespeare Company production of *Desert Air* at The Other Place, where stars and minor players test their skills in eyeball-to-eyeball proximity with the small audience. Having been warned about the rigours of the virtually unheated ex-factory building, Simon came fortified with a thermos flask of hot lemon and whisky, and occasional sips from it helped to engender an atmosphere closer to the play's theme of World War II action in the North African desert.

During the winter, we had seized upon the closeness of our Lapworth base to Stratford to see as many productions of this great company as possible. There had been the thoughtful, yet unemotional, performance of Roger Rees in *Hamlet*: the season's triumph in Anthony Sher's dramatic, exaggeratedly crippled *Richard III*; and finally, *Love's Labours Lost*, staged rather like a Chekhov play.

After the performance we would often adjourn to the Dirty Duck (which serves as the RSC's green room) where the actors and actresses from the night's productions at either place rub shoulders, easily and unselfconsciously, with the audience. The pub stands above a stone wall opposite the garden beyond the west end of the Memorial Theatre. On the town and tourist side the sign denotes 'The White Swan'; on the other side, 'The Dirty Duck'. The walls of the bar are packed layer upon layer with autographed photos of the great stars, past and present: Laurence Olivier, John Gielgud, Ralph Richardson, Albert Finney, Peggy Ashcroft, Anna Massey. It is regarded as a signal honour to be asked to join their ranks.

Back at Lapworth on the boat there was a different style of entertainment. Mornings usually started with ribald exchanges across the separating stretch of frozen canal as Eric made his regular check on conditions.

'You're still around then?' he shouted as I appeared bleary-eyed after a late return from the Dirty Duck the previous evening.

'Why? Any problems? It looks about the same around this stagnating backwater as always.'

'No. No, there're no problems, now that you've decided to emerge and rejoin our society,' he replied in a flat, innocent voice. 'I sorted out all the problems last night while you were away gallivanting. Nothing serious to worry about – just a load of kids bringing a boat down through the lock. I told them not to worry about that abandoned boat over there – just keep clear of mine. I said, "That boat belongs to those people who come and dump it here in the winter while they go off to the sun in Spain."'

'Great. Thanks for looking after everything so well,' I retorted. 'It's a nice place here apart from the noisy, troublesome neighbours.'

Ruth appeared from *Sandalwood*'s sidehatch, looking a little perplexed about the raucous shouting, and signalled that she was coming across the lock to talk to us. She arrived, Dan bouncing alongside.

'Big Teddy! Big Teddy!' demanded Dan.

Lynda fetched the giant teddy bear, with its golden fleece and warm brown eyes, our mascot, that had tolerantly accompanied us through our travels. Dan rolled over him on the sofa.

'Don't worry about Eric – he's a bit excited today as it's his birthday,' Ruth told us, conspiratorially.

At teatime we went across to *Sandalwood*, where Eric sat in state while Ruth produced a magnificent homemade chocolate cake, crowned by a single candle.

A few days later, it was Dan's second birthday. For him, Ruth had manufactured an ingenious replica of a steam engine – the boiler made from a Swiss roll, the cabin from a coloured sponge, the wheels from slices of miniature chocolate rolls. There were two candles for funnels, and it was decorated with jellies. Dan, after much coaching, succeeded in extinguishing the candles in one mighty blow.

Real steam trains returned to the Leamington–Paddington line about this time. On Sundays, they were inserted into the normal service, as an experiment to test their appeal to enthusiasts and tourists. Passing over the bridge that crossed our arm of the canal, the Lord Raglan pulled two elegant Victorian observer coaches, followed another day by the Flying Scotsman. It became a regular feature of Sundays to hear the countryside echoing with the haunting, evocative whistle of a steam engine as it puffed and huffed its way up the hill alongside Hatton flight and roared past the Lapworth basin, photographers and sightseers clustering at good viewing points.

Moored as we were in close proximity to another residential boat, there was a convention in the morning that there would be no unnecessary calling until the curtains were drawn back, rather like the old boater's practice of keeping the hatches shut. For our part, we tried to avoid calling on *Sandalwood* during the afternoon, when Eric took a rest while Dan, who could be very demanding at other times, slept.

Some dark mornings in the rich wood of the stern cabin, we would oversleep until Margaret, taking her mid-morning walk, would shout raucously, 'Wake up, you lazybones! I've brought your post.' She was invariably dressed elegantly, more for the city than the country, from an endless range of dresses, fur coats and stylish hats.

Over a cup of coffee, or preferably a mid-day glass of whisky, she would regale us with inexhaustible stories of her single-handed exploits in every part of the waterways. Having lived afloat for some five or six years, there were few places that she had not visited, and she had had many interesting encounters with other boating people, recorded in personal messages in the 'Visitors' Book' that she kept.

Despite the near-impossible conditions for outside work, the local BWB team were endeavouring to carry out their repairs to the north Stratford flight. We were full of admiration for their individual efforts, yet wondered whether BWB had adopted the right policy for concentrating maintenance into a period of the year unsuited to this work. One day, walking to Potterton's, we witnessed the strange sight of BWB men trying to shaft an unpowered flat, loaded with equipment, through thick ice, strenuously smashing a narrow passage to bring it to their work place.

On *Frederick*, our own consultancy work was intensified, as we were keen to make use of this period of immobility by increasing our earnings, and there were few weeks when either Lynda or I did not travel to London on the excellent Birmingham International InterCity service. Around the middle of February, Lynda had to go for two days and, taking over one of her regular chores of mopping the sides and roof of the stern cabin, I was amazed to discover the scale of overnight condensation.

We had started to notice several days earlier this worsening situation, which we put down to two main factors: the lack of any separating door between the kitchen – with drifting steam from evening cooking – and the bedroom, together with inadequate heating (only a small floor-level radiator) at the stern.

The morning after returning from London, Lynda stepped out of bed into a pool of cold water. In a state of panic, we discovered that water was lying about an inch deep over the carpet in the far corner of the cabin where there was an inspection hatch to the bilge. Troubles never come singly. Staggering after her down the length of the boat I found that the main saloon, normally comfortably warm from a banked-up overnight fire, was freezing cold. For the first time in many weeks, just when we needed it most, the Parkray stove had let us down.

Living on water, naturally, our first reaction had been that we must have sprung a leak in the hull, perhaps caused by the pressure of the ice. Although it was unlikely in such a new, well-built hull, examined in dry dock only six months previously, it seemed the obvious explanation for the stern cabin flood, and when you live on water there is always a lingering fear of sinking.

There was no sign, however, that the boat was dropping. An immediate check outside confirmed that the hull was sitting at its normal level. The next check on the propeller tube – the only orifice below water level – was also reassuring. No problems there, so from where was the water coming? Before trying to work out the source, however, we had to deal with the effect.

While Lynda started to bale out by the bucketful from under the bed, I cleared and cleaned the stove. It was not surprising that it had failed: the fuel basket was blocked deeply with enormous lumps of twisted clinker. During the cold patch, there had been no chance to let out the fire and give it a thorough cleaning and brushing of the flues.

'What's going on over there? It's too early for spring-cleaning,' Eric shouted from *Sandalwood*. 'Have you got a fire or a leak?'

'No, we haven't got a fire of any sort!! But I think we've got a leak!!!'

Eric came on board to help, first tranferring the pump from the stern bilge to the point beneath the bed so that the area was soon emptied of water. Now we were faced with the immense task of clearing the bedroom in order to lift and remove the carpet, which was totally sodden.

There is not much space on a narrowboat for this kind of exercise. The large window on the bank side was taken out of its wooden frame and we lifted the pine chest-of-drawers through it – as it had been delivered onto the boat last May from an Oxford shop. The high bed had provided a marvellous opportunity for storing many different items beneath it – suitcases, spare clothing, surplus timber, unfinished patchwork and magazines – which were now transferred to other cabins, then the double mattress squeezed down the corridor, blocking access. Now the thick green carpet, nailed around the sides on an underlay of foam rubber, was lifted, rolled from one side, the bed transferred to the cleared section, the remaining carpet rolled and then tied together.

Having absorbed gallons of water, the carpet was enormously heavy. We managed to eject it through the window and trundle it on a wheelbarrow to Eric's workshop, where it was strung on ropes from the roof and, dripping, left to dry in the warmth of a fan heater. From the depths of Eric's workshop, stacked with discarded items retained for potential future needs, an old industrial heater was produced, plugged into *Frederick*'s 240V generator system, and the lengthy task of drying out the boat was begun.

'At least you're not sinking,' Eric said as we sat, recovering, over Ruth's welcome mugs of hot coffee. 'So, in that case, where is the water coming from, Dr Watson?'

'I've checked the stern tube and I can't believe that this hull has sprung a leak,' I pondered. 'So, that's the problem. What's the answer, Holmes?'

'The solution is simple, my dear Watson. Consider the following fact that I have observed: the water in the bilge is clear and clean.'

'You mean – not dirty enough to have come from the canal?'

'Correct.'

'So?'

'So, it must have come from inside the boat. We had better start looking for a leaking pipe.'

The search commenced at the bows, where there was another bilge inspection hatch immediately below the three water tanks, holding up to 450 gallons. At this point it was dry. Further along the boat we found that the carpets and floorboards in the study and corridor were wet, and they were rolled back to dry out as they were not so bad that they needed lifting.

We removed the facia panels around the central core of the domestic water system, the header tank and calorifier, situated between the kitchen and bathroom, and from the side of the bath. There was no obvious fault, but we could not see into the most inaccessible part around the hot-water tank: this wall was solid. However, I could detect a steady dripping of water in this part and noticed steam rising.

There was no alternative but to cut an inspection hole through the bathroom wall. On checking the construction diagrams, we discovered that it was a hazardous spot where, inevitably, there were several pipes which we could not see. Calculating the minimum effective entrance and drawing the outline on the wall, Eric prepared to cut with a powered jig saw.

'I don't like doing this one bit,' he remarked as he braced himself to make the first cut like a surgeon at a major operation.

From the opposite side, through a minute gap over the top of the cooker, I watched intently for any sudden, undesired spurt from a severed artery. It did not come; the operation was completed. When we removed the small panel, the saw had grazed past several pipes, and the source of the malady was open to view, a weeping wound at the top of the calorifier, a steady seepage that must have been festering for some time.

A new section of brass pipe was obtained to replace the faulty plastic one, turned to shape and a stop tap added to help any future difficulties – all of this plumbing carried out under the most awkward circumstances of working through the small hole on the bathroom wall. The repair held and the leak was stemmed. This problem had been solved within a day. The drying out of the cabin took much longer, however; we lived, somewhat uncomfortably, in the bare boarded bedroom for two weeks before the carpet was sufficiently dry to be relaid, when we had to go right through the whole laborious process of moving furniture again. Finally, we were back to normal; the accident that we had experienced would not have been unusual on land, yet somehow it had not been expected when living on water.

As conditions inside the boat improved, so the weather outside began to change. Around the end of February there were several brilliantly clear days when warmth returned to the sun and the deep snow started to melt and ebb away. Although temperatures overnight dropped to below zero, keeping the canal frozen over, the sun began to win the battle and green shoots emerged through the blanket of snow. After weeks of total, overall whiteness, it was a relief to see other colours appearing in the landscape: there had been a pure beauty in the frozen scene, yet this had become monotonous after a time. We were able to walk again down the Stratford canal, across fields still partially covered with a scree of ebbing snow, and up a bridle path, now a rushing stream, to Lapworth church. The heavily pregnant buds of spring were ready to burst into life.

Almost unnoticed, the days were lengthening. One evening, at 6 p.m., in the red glow of sunset I was sitting on a lock beam wearing only a sweater over my shirt. Below, soft ice was still floating around *Sandalwood* and *Frederick*, and snow was lying in crevices hidden from the sunlight.

'It's been a hard winter, perhaps the hardest that I've known in Lapworth,' Eric ruminated. 'Yet it's a funny thing, once the better spring weather arrives, you quickly forget the hard times. In this country even a severe winter lasts only for a few weeks, though at the time it seems endless. Soon the change happens, like today, and here in the country, in the open, we know and experience these first feelings of spring.'

My own thoughts were turning to plans for moving on, now that the BWB winter stoppage programme was due to end shortly.

I checked the level of the diesel tanks – last filled at Aylesbury – and found that they were down to less than fifteen gallons. With the way to the north still closed, our nearest point of supply was in Warwick on the far side of Hatton flight. I telephoned Kate Boats who confirmed that they might have sufficient to meet our needs.

John and Penny arrived from London on Friday evening for their first weekend since New Year's Eve. When I explained the situation, there was no question about how we should spend the time.

'A great excuse – we'll go to Warwick and back,' both of them exclaimed.

'You're sure? You mean – all the way down Hatton, twenty-three locks to the Cape and back?'

'Absolutely certain. It'll be a splendid way of getting going again after the winter, banish blues, limber up the muscles. Just imagine how mad everyone else will think we are!'

The Saturday morning was bright and sunny, but by the time the boat had been prepared for moving and we had told the Hunts what we were doing it was twelve noon before we set out.

After months of immobility it was thrilling to be gliding along the smooth waters of the Grand Union, past Tom o'the Woods, through Rowington cutting and Shrewley tunnel, a hasty lunch stop at the top of Hatton since the days were still short, then a record descent in two and a half hours with the four of us working in unison. Halfway down, we were excited to meet another boat on the ascent, which meant that we had some locks in our favour.

The next morning, we continued through the two locks at Cape of Good Hope on the edge of Warwick and at the boatyard filled the tanks with eighty gallons of diesel, nearly exhausting their own reserves.

On the return ascent of Hatton, we had been making excellent going when Lynda – who had disappeared from sight, opening locks far ahead of the boat – returned. She was looking very worried.

'I don't know how to put this,' she exclaimed, 'but the top pound and lock are completely dry!'

'Go on – it's a leg pull – you must be joking.'

'No. No, seriously – I'm afraid that they may be doing some more maintenance work.'

She convinced me enough to go and see for myself. I found that it was true. The pound that we had passed through only twenty-four hours earlier was now totally dry, down to a small stream trickling along the muddy bottom. Being a Sunday, it seemed possible that it had been drained in preparation for work on Monday. I went to check at the lockkeeper's cottage.

'No, there's nothing planned,' I was told. 'There have been one or two boats through the flight and someone must have left up a paddle. Can you fill it yourself?'

It is not an uncommon occurrence on the canals, yet it was our first actual experience of it. By the time I returned to the top lock, another boat had arrived ready to descend equally bewildered by the scene.

'Are you the lockkeeper?' they asked.

'No, but I'm acting for him,' I replied.

Opening up the top and bottom paddles, the water surged through the lock, rushing torrentially into the hollow pound and quickly filling it. It gave one quite a sensation of power, coupled with a realisation, like never before, of the inherent dangers in the waterways and of the responsibility that should be recognised by all users to ensure correct and safe operation.

We returned to Lapworth just before dark, some eighteen hours, forty-six locks and eighteen miles after leaving it, our muscles screaming from their unaccustomed use, yet deeply satisfied at achieving such a successful, enjoyable start to travelling in the new year.

Now we began to prepare in earnest for our return to a travelling way of life. The diesel tanks had been filled. Next, we stocked up with solid fuel and propane gas while we were within reach of the local facilities. We bought food supplies while we still had use of the car. We made plans for our route, heading first to Stoke-on-Trent and the Caldon canal. A call to BWB's area engineer confirmed that the Grand Union was open to Birmingham, but the mainline to Wolverhampton was still closed.

'You could get to the Caldon along the Fazeley link to the Trent and Mersey,' he explained, then added in a tone of voice implying that no one in their right mind would attempt it, 'and, of course, the northern loop is open, if you want to tackle *that*.'

Studying the map, we found that a long, tortuous section of the Birmingham Canal Navigation provided a route from Salford to Wolverhampton, passing through Walsall, close to Norton Canes where *Frederick* had been built at Malcolm Braine's yard. We decided that it would be a fitting way to begin the next stage of the journey.

Chapter Six

Breakdown

The dim, chilly light of a morning in late March was shattered by the harsh clang of an alarm clock. It was 7 a.m. on the day that we were setting out on our travels again after the long winter sojourn, and there were hours of hard work ahead. From our overnight mooring in the last patch of country on the fringe of Solihull, we planned to pass through the centre of Birmingham and arrive at a more isolated spot (we did not know precisely where) by nightfall.

After months of relative inactivity, it was sad to part from the company and support of Eric and Ruth, and we felt a shade apprehensive about leaving the friendly comforts of an environment that we knew so well, a place where we had become identified with the community, a mooring where we were aware of small local problems and sensitive to any change in water conditions. Just as sick people become institutionalised after a long period, reassured by concerned nurses and respected doctors, reliant on the disciplined routine to which they have become accustomed, so for Lynda and me it was curiously unnerving to move away from the balm of the Warwickshire countryside towards a vast amorphous city, notorious for its industrial dereliction and the accompanying ravages of vandalism, travelling along waterways completely unknown to us at an early stage in the season when it was unlikely that many other boats would be around.

Our immediate objective within two days was to reach Norton Canes, near Walsall, and the boatbuilding yard of Malcolm Braine – the maker of *Frederick*. Then, after a short break, to continue along the tortuous and little-used northern loop of the BCN to Wolverhampton, dropping down the twenty-one-lock flight on to the Staffordshire and Worcestershire canal at Aldersley junction where, from the map, it appeared that we would emerge from the sprawling urbanisation of the West Midlands into the countryside of Staffordshire.

Before setting out on such a long, difficult section of the waterways I always summarised the route in terms of miles and locks to give us a rough guide of what we had to accomplish and what rate of progress we should be seeking. Now we knew that we had a further eight miles and six locks on the Grand Union to Bordesley junction, followed by five miles and thirteen locks to the Rushall canal, where the northern loop started. Then, about thirty miles and thirty locks to Aldersley, including the diversion to Norton Canes. The total of forty-three miles and forty-nine locks was fairly typical of the lock/mile ratio on the Midlands canals, although the locks were grouped together in flights with long pounds between them.

After this, we had a tentative plan for the rest of the summer, but it was not fixed to any precise time schedule. We had originally set out on a twelve-month sabbatical for the duration of the rental of our London house, but the tenant, who had proved to be ideal, had asked for a further six months extension, to which we agreed. It enabled us to look ahead to the whole spring, summer and autumn period for unrestricted boating without the need to impose a time limit on any particular section – we could stop where we pleased for as long as we wished, and continue again roughly in the direction we had planned.

There was an overall strategy. Our first target after joining the Staffs and Worcs canal was to travel along the Trent and Mersey to Stoke-on-Trent, turning up the Caldon which we had tried to reach two years earlier from Braunston in *Hanover* and failed to achieve in a two-week round trip. Beyond here, the Macclesfield canal on the edge of the Peak District appealed, as well as the great Shropshire Union crossing the Cheshire plain. Then I needed to return down the river Severn to research a magazine feature linked with the projected plan to extend its navigation beyond the present limit at Stourport. The Gloucester and Sharpness ship canal could be a possibility if we wanted to travel to the most south-westerly extent of the system. At this stage in March, we envisaged reaching Sharpness by mid-summer, leaving open the opportunity of going to the northern limit of York, which was Lynda's own personal ambition.

Now we were on day one, setting out to Birmingham – not a part of our route to which I felt strongly attracted as I had given up my working career to retreat from the big city scene. Not everyone feels the same way: many boaters have an intense interest in the industrial archaeology of such places. I recall one occasion ascending Hatton flight in the company of another boat skippered by a West Country farmer, for whom the high point of his holiday was passing through Birmingham – a complete change for him from fields and animals.

The route of the Grand Union into Britain's second largest city turned out to be as surprising as a magician's sleight of hand. The canal proceeded through a deep, wide cutting with pleasant tree-lined slopes that hid the sprawling mass of dense suburban housing that had been familiar to me from the roads on business trips. On the boat, we remained in a semi-rural vacuum until close to the city centre.

The morning had brightened from its early dull, misty start and sunshine filtered through the wintry bare branches, picking out the brilliant electric-blue flight of two kingfishers that accompanied us for some distance, swooping and darting over the water, a sudden flash of lightning that disappeared into bushes, re-emerging into another startling explosion of colour. One of the birds perched for long enough to surprise us with its bright orange breast. There is no more exciting colouring in Britain's bird life.

The illusion faded around Tyseley, a point well remembered by the old boatmen as they reached the outpost of wharves and warehouses, satisfied at reaching their destination, perhaps after an exhausting non-stop journey from Brentford in less than sixty hours. The area now offered mixed scenery: many fine old brick warehouses (now mostly shut and decaying, though here and there one was being restored), while other former commercial sites had been razed to the ground, sometimes replaced by the anonymous blank face of modern factories.

Little advantage was being taken of the canal environment until the mainline railway bridge, where a valiant attempt was being made to landscape the surroundings with turfed slopes, newly planted trees and winding paths. Along here, work was going on to improve the condition of the towing-path. In the thick network of dull streets I spotted a once grand, ornate Victorian building, ingeniously patterned in brick, surmounted by a cupola. Further in the distance ahead could be seen the cluster of high modern concrete blocks in the centre of Birmingham.

The wide and reasonably clean canal terminated at Bordesley, the limit of the improvements carried out in the 1930s, and we descended through six narrowbeam locks as high walls enclosed the sides and the canal disappeared into a cavernous passage under criss-crossing roads and railway bridges carrying the resounding roar of heavy traffic.

Halfway down Camp Hill flight another boat appeared, ascending, and warned us about the difficulties of the bottom lock, where they had spent about two hours trying to free it of rubbish. Although their passage had cleared it partially, we still needed two attempts before *Frederick* was through; on the first, the hull became wedged immovably by the sides of a child's plastic pedal car. This was one of our worst experiences so far of the way in which some city-dwellers regard canals (which often provide their only potential leisure and environmental lung) as the nearest, most convenient rubbish dump.

At the foot of the flight, we turned sharply right, under one of the perfectly proportioned roving bridges built by Horseley Iron Works that give a characteristic feature to the BCN, and into the Saltley canal, a two-mile link to Salford junction. We had arrived in a landscape totally dominated by industry and commerce from which almost all natural life and human habitation had been banished, and dereliction was widespread. The immense fat towers of a power station belched pollution over this depressing scenery, where some factories struggled on while others had simply given up and died.

The canal itself was so full of plastic bags, supermarket trolleys and sinister-looking objects that *Frederick* seemed almost to be floating on a layer of refuse through which murky, thick liquid oozed. I am told that it is not always so foul. This section lay at the foot of flights emptying from the city centre and, as we were one of the first boats through after the winter closures, all the detritus had collected and was yet to be flushed away by the passage of other craft.

At Salford junction, there was the option of turning right along the Birmingham and Fazeley canal towards more open country at Tamworth, but we held to our plan, turning left and going deeper still into the West Midlands conurbation. First, we encountered one of the modern wonders of transport – Spaghetti Junction.

From the road one cannot appreciate fully the complexity of this motorway madness, where several different roads intersect with the M6 in creating the most elaborate interwoven pattern in Britain, making mockery of a plate of pasta. It is from the comparative peace of the canal, built more than a hundred years earlier, that the finest – or worst – view is obtained. Although I had driven into Birmingham on this route many times, I had never before fully comprehended the way in which tier upon tier of suspended concrete road is interleaved, supported by massive pillars rising from the canal itself. As we plodded along, a single boat isolated from the frenzied activity above, vehicles careered in every direction overhead as though on some never-ending rollercoaster. Chugging along at a sedate 4 m.p.h., crossing a river, we were detached enough to marvel at how road-planners ever achieved such intricate patterns.

A pair of locks lifted us away from Spaghetti Junction and into the Tame Valley, where an old man took pride in pointing out the difference in the paddle gear: there was a two-sided spindle to the ratchet, as on the Worcester and Birmingham canal, so that two people could work it together. Above the locks, we found ourselves in the first relatively quiet spot since entering Birmingham, and nine hours after starting from Solihull we stopped for a late, late lunch, feeling weary from such unaccustomed activity and battered by the extreme changes of scene.

We could not afford to stop for long: there were the thirteen Perry Bar locks ahead and we aimed to tie for the night at the top, if conditions seemed suitable. The flight lifted us above the heavy industry of Salford valley, each lock taking us a stage further away from the steaming, smoky cauldron of factories and the power station, the vast blocks of Fort Dunlop diminishing in scale as we rose above them. Further along the flight, buildings fell away on either side leaving some open land around the canal and giving a view to the south, across an extensive sports and leisure complex, of the tower blocks, like a mini Chicago, of central Birmingham.

Rain was starting to fall lightly as we ascended the last lock, and the keeper assured us that there was comparatively safe overnight mooring beyond the high road bridge. We found that there was indeed a secluded cutting, just out of sight of houses and the busy road, and gratefully settled there for the night, some twelve hours after setting out and twenty-six locks further on. We crashed out and were asleep soon after 10 p.m.

The alarm was set for 7 a.m. the next morning. Again, there was another long, demanding day ahead of us in trying to reach Norton Canes. It turned out, however, to be a day of fascinating contrast, not quite so depressing as the previous day.

As with the situation twenty-four hours before, when we were approaching Birminghan, the Tame Valley canal came as a pleasant surprise, passing through a deep cutting with bridges soaring remotely overhead, then running along an embankment where grassy commonland separated it from the housing estates below. Opened in 1844, one of the last major canals to be built in Britain, its appearance is altogether more modern – straight, wide, deep, with firm sides and a towing-path along both banks. In its day, it had been constructed like a twentieth-century motorway to by-pass the long delays caused by the congested and outdated Farmers Bridge and Aston flights, comprising twenty-four locks.

The Tame Valley canal came too late, however; it had been opened only a short time before traffic started to decline as the railways took over. Until then a complex and confusing network of waterways had been built throughout the West Midlands, providing a variety of alternative routes to meet surging demand from Stour-bridge in the south-west to Brownhills on the opposite side, and Wolverhampton in the north-west to Birmingham via Dudley and Smethwick. At its peak there were 160 miles of Birmingham Canal Navigation, though it was never a properly planned and integrated system since three companies were involved in bitter rivalry to attract traffic. Although many fringe routes have been lost in the past fifty years, 100 miles of BCN remain and it is said that Birmingham has more miles of canal than Venice.

Passing under the flyover where the M5 and M6 divided, we turned into the Rushall canal through another of the elegant Victorian iron bridges with its characteristic geometric pattern. We had entered the long, winding, northern loop of BCN canals which come under the BWB 'remainder' category. Under the Transport Act of 1968 waterways were divided into two categories: those which were more heavily used and would be maintained to operating level, and other 'remainder' sections which would be kept open as long as there was some demand for them, depending of course on other local factors.

We found the bottom lock of the Rushall flight of nine was dry, but the keeper was already in the process of filling it. He told me that the paddles had been raised by vandals, a not infrequent event. 'That's the problem around here, far too many kids from the housing estates with nothing to do but look for trouble,' he explained.

I remarked on the good appearance of the flight – the initial impression seemed far better than expected – of this remainder canal: indeed, conditions looked superior to many more popular routes.

'It's all right, I suppose, nothing wrong with it, but it's a boring place to work,' he replied. 'Even in the peak season there's no more than one boat a day through here. I can't see why they keep it going – there's no interest in this canal.'

The keeper helped us through the flight as far as lock seven, where he retreated to his house for a cup of tea. At the top, we found a gang of youths working on towpath improvements, presumably under a MSC scheme. Although it was a routine job, they seemed to be cheerful and enjoying it, and they shouted encouragements as *Frederick* passed by, pleased to see a boat on the move.

Around Daw End, about a mile further on, the rolling green country and a charming canalside pub reminded us briefly of the delights of the Oxford canal. It did not last. Through Aldridge and Brownhills the canal was never far from housing estates and industry, though here the factories were more modern and a hive of activity. Communities were interspersed with patchy scrubland; at one point we passed above a moonscape of subsided mines, raw earth and stone collapsing into deep glassy pools, and beyond, distant views of tower blocks and cooling towers.

Progress through this unattractive scenery seemed slow as the cut was incredibly tortuous and so shallow that we had to keep to the middle: maintaining the water level must be a problem since the long lock-free pound stretches the entire way from Rushall to Wolverhampton.

At last, by about 5 p.m. and far later than I had anticipated, we reached Pelsall junction and turned right into the Cannock connection, the last BCN navigation to be built in 1858, originally providing a direct link to the Staffs and Worcs canal at Hatherton but abandoned in 1954, little surviving beyond Norton Canes. The next two miles were memorable: from a low, smoke-blackened brick bridge at the junction we could see down the dead-straight canal, crossed at regular intervals by black bridges, creating a three-dimensional effect and a sense of mystery reminiscent of a scene from a moody Italian film. A bare heathland was backed at the far end by a dark wood of leafless trees. It was our first glimpse of open country since leaving Warwickshire two days earlier. .

We found boating life again on a side arm where a pair of working boats and other craft were moored beneath the derelict remains of a red-brick Victorian warehouse, once a flourishing coal wharf. Beyond, we came upon a group of low buildings bearing the name of M. E. Braine (Boatbuilder), edged past a cluster of handsome narrowboats, nudged out of the way an odd hybrid boat called *Atlantis* (we learned later that it had been specially built for a film), and squeezed into a mooring for the night.

Malcolm Braine soon appeared, a sprightly figure in blue overalls, shouting a welcome across the intervening water, and eventually he came over to join us for a glass of wine on board *Frederick* – his maker had arrived!

Long before buying *Frederick* we had admired the acknowledged styling of Braine boats: their overall appearance was strong and sturdy, yet the flowing lines of the cabin, distinctively sweeping upwards towards the stern, was evocative of the finest original working craft. People with an eye for narrowboats easily spot the design, as we have learned from frequent enquiries: 'Is that a Malcolm Braine boat?' Now, at Norton Canes, *Frederick* gave an aura of contentment, floating among his family of unmistakable pedigree. 'It's like a stud farm,' Lynda remarked.

It is not surprising that Malcolm has been accorded this recognition since he was among the first of the new generation of builders to begin converting former working narrowboats for the new leisure purposes, and there was a time when he achieved an outstanding reputation for some of his most successful conversions. One of them, a steam-powered boat called *President*, is on show at the Black Country Museum at Tipton. Although others have followed, Malcolm Braine's place in the history of boatbuilding in the new waterways era is assured.

There had been a time when Malcolm himself lived afloat so we talked, as boaters do when they gather together, of past experiences. We quizzed him about the hazardous Trent Falls on the river Ouse that has to be crossed to reach York, and he reassured us that the difficulties, though real, were exaggerated by some. He recalled his most frightening incident on the waterways, when he was steering a narrowboat on the tidal Thames below Tower Bridge and it was passed by a hovercraft, creating a trough six feet deep.

'I saw that the bow was passing over the top of the wave and realised that it was going to plunge down into the trough. I couldn't believe that there was any chance of it returning upright before it would be engulfed. This, I thought was going to be the ultimate moment when the bow would dig under the water and for a few terrifying seconds I believed that I had lost the boat. Somehow, it shuddered out of the situation and returned to level.'

We asked him about the current state of the business.

'There's no pleasure any longer in boatbuilding, what with staff and delivery problems, inflating prices. My only enjoyment is from meeting people who have my boats and talking with them about their experiences. Sadly, I've no longer any time left for boating; that's what I would like to get back to.'

Since we met him, Malcolm has handed over his business to one of his own employees, so perhaps he is now returning to active boating.

The next day we walked around the yard, admiring the work of skilled craftsmen. There was the steel shell of a full-length boat, the bows carefully shaped to replicate the high, wide prow of the Joshua working boats. Alongside, a new boat was just being started, its base plate laid out with its stem post standing upright, yet to be moulded, like the aggressive bow of a Norse longboat. Dedicated care was being given to the renovation of an elegant forty-foot wooden cruiser, built at Bourne in Lincolnshire in 1967, which the Chairman of BWB, Sir Leslie Young, was coming to inspect later in the day.

Absorbed in the activity, we fell behind in our own intended departure and scrambled away at lunchtime, not stopping to eat, Malcolm waving farewell as we set off. 'If you ever have any problems, just call for help,' he shouted.

He warned us not to stop overnight anywhere in Wolverhampton, which has a bad record for vandalism, except in the basin at the top of the flight, but we had underestimated the distance and difficulties of the journey. The boatyard had been sheltered, so we had not appreciated the fierce wind that was blowing until we started to battle against it along the Pelsall arm. At the junction – turning into the splendidly named Wyrley and Essington – we hit the full force which made it extremely difficult to steer along the narrow, shallow canal. Then, in a particularly exposed place, the engine suddenly cut out without warning and *Frederick* was blown on to the side.

It could have been a mechanical failure; on the other hand, a substantial object caught and wound around the propeller could have caused the same result. In the back of the engine room, groping in the darkness under the stern counter, I delved into the weed hatch, first unscrewing the large wing nuts that hold the steel plate in place, then lifting it so that I could feel around the propeller underwater. Although the weed hatch is a marvellous device in giving access to this vital part of the boat, it is not pleasant to search around in cold murky water, wondering about what horrible object may have become entwined.

Sure enough, I could feel a large piece of fabric wound tightly around the propeller shaft. Stage by stage, I hacked away with a sharp knife, removing chunks of blue cloth until I could free the propeller sufficiently to turn it by hand and unwind the rest, pulling out the remains of an anorak. It could have been worse: I have seen other boaters dealing with a fisherman's keepnet and mattress springs, among other objects. Even so, we had lost some sixty minutes of valuable time in this tiresome operation, at a time of the year when darkness descended by about 6 p.m., and it took several minutes of exhausting effort to push the boat underway from the side against the force of the wind.

School had finished by the time we reached a modern spacious housing estate and teenagers were romping from a fine comprehensive set in playing fields – no dereliction around this place. They gathered on a newly built footbridge over the canal, seeming to show an interest in this comparatively rare sight of a full-length narrowboat passing along the canal. Lynda was steering and she was greeted by a hail of pebbles, spit and abuse.

It was an unnerving experience since by now there were many lithe, tall youths roaming along the towing-path, some carrying air rifles, others throwing stones idly into the cut. At each bridge, we saw faces peering over the sides. On the boat, we wondered what devilish tricks they were planning and we felt exposed, chugging along at two or three miles per hour, often at bridges close to the sides. As a precaution, I put the hammer and mooring spikes within hands' reach, but it was unnecessary. We had no further incidents: indeed, many of the young people called out friendly enquiring remarks. It is the shame of modern urban society that a few culprits create such a bad reputation for their generation and cause anxieties which, at times, may prevent better interchange.

The geography of this canal was extraordinary in that we followed a sweeping loop from Rushall up to Pelsall and then returned down the other side so that at one point we were only a mile or two away across country from Daw End. There was another change of direction at Sneyd junction, where a sharp turn brought us south-west towards Wolverhampton, now passing through open parkland on the city's outskirts.

As industrial buildings once again enclosed the canal sides and we could discern the tower blocks of the city centre, dusk was falling so rapidly that I started to worry whether we would reach our destination, but the surrounding dereliction and unwelcome atmosphere encouraged us to press on. The cut became twisting, sharp turns and obstructions barely picked out by the headlight's beam, a startling eerie glimpse into the turgid black water of a side arm, deep unfathomable shadows of gaunt, lifeless warehouses, the putative threat of colliding with some unseen, unknown object.

Then, suddenly, joyfully, the bow nudged out of the tortuous canal into a wider area, the junction with the mainline Birmingham route, and I knew that we could not be far from the basin. Edging around the turning, we continued under a series of bridges that created a tunnel, the black outline of the spans supporting office buildings that towered above us like the walls of a canyon, floor upon floor brilliantly illuminated, the myriad lights of traffic like fireflies darting overhead. The dark Satanic mills of Blake's Jerusalem came to mind, though here we were far from England's green and pleasant land. Groping along the deepest, darkest tunnel, we emerged, thankfully, into the glowing warmth of the basin, reassured by twinkling lights from other boats, smoke curling from their chimneys.

A week later – after travelling up the northern half of the Staffs and Worcs and on the Trent and Mersey from Great Haywood – we arrived in Stoke-on-Trent. At Etruria lock a group of early Victorian buildings in mellow purple brick with wide arched windows were as elegant as chapels or schools, yet tapering brick chimneys confirmed that they made up one of the former flint-mills that had contributed so much to the wealth of Stoke's ceramic business. Contrasted with the vast, faceless, featureless prison blocks of modern industry, it seemed impossible that these stylish buildings dating from 1857 could have once been a place of work.

The light rain that had started as a drizzle in the early afternoon, had steadily thickened until the vaporous clouds seemed to merge into the land and turned into a downpour. There is nothing quite to equal the total, engulfing depression of a wet day in a northern English industrial city. When the first shower started we had donned waterproof coats with hoods, then, as the rain intensified, we had put on leggings outside rubber boots so that underneath this protective clothing we were dry as we sploshed around the locks. On the bank watching us intently, was a pale, thin young man, clutching a plastic bag, his anorak saturated, somehow conveying an impression that he would like to join us.

Martin came on board, stood next to me on the counter and warned me about the extraordinarily sharp turns and low bridges of the Caldon canal, particularly a notorious lift bridge. I recruited him as a crew member. The first turn above Etruria brought the boat around so that it was facing back towards the lovely group of Victorian buildings, and then we arrived on the Caldon, thus achieving our first target in the year's programme. Ahead, I could see the two-lock staircase which lifted the canal on its way into the Peak District and, arriving into a small pool, we again made an angular turn, coaxing *Frederick* around so that we could start to ascend.

In the first of the two locks Martin told me that mining subsidence had caused the bottom to drop so much that many years ago a working boat loaded with flint had sunk there and never been retrieved. Somewhere, underneath us, it lay, rotting in the mud.

'You seem to know a lot about the Caldon – how's that?' I asked.

'Me dad, 'e's a boatman – 'e runs the noo working boats oop there. You'll likely see 'im, or at any rate, 'is boats,' Martin replied. 'Me dad, 'e works oop and dawn 'ere every day, and some days I give 'im a hand. I love to do it.'

Above the roar of the engine and the insulation of my waterproof hood it was difficult to hear what Martin was saying, but his enthusiasm for the canal was so infectious that I passed over the steering of *Frederick* to him as we approached the extremely low bridges he had warned about. The canal was the most tortuous that we had yet experienced; it looped among mellow brick Victorian buildings, sadly now deserted, and reached a bridge so low that I had to leap off the boat and carry the TV aerial. *Frederick* just skimmed underneath. Martin was right also about the struggle over the lift bridge: both of us ran ahead, Lynda steering, and it took our combined efforts to raise it.

A little further on we passed, tied on a wharf outside a pottery factory, a pair of modern blue flat boats, designed so that stacks of ceramics could be wheeled straight on to them, and I gathered that this was Harold's work, transporting them backwards and forwards between one production centre and another. To us it was an exciting moment, to see the first pair of boats, albeit modern, actually involved in a commercial operation that we had yet come across.

When he first came on board Martin had refused my offer of waterproof clothing, or my suggestion of taking shelter in the cabin with a hot cup of coffee. I gathered that he had no regular employment but had taught himself to paint traditional roses and castles on boats and gained some work this way. It seemed disappointing that the regeneration of English waterways could not have found a place for someone with Martin's intense personal enthusiasm for them.

We parted on the outside edge of Hanley. Martin jumped off the boat to return to Stoke by bus, rejecting my offer to pay his fare, a sadly drenched figure disappearing into the damp gloom. We bid farewell, as always in this travelling life, by saying that we would be returning in a few days and perhaps we would meet again.

The next morning, Good Friday – after eating Hot Cross buns bought in Stone which were awarded the 'best ever' commendation – we started to climb the Stockton Brook flight, set in pleasant semi-rural surroundings. Further enthusiastic help came from two young lads, aged about ten or twelve, who announced proudly that they were Boy Scouts: 'We've been taught how to help people, carefully,' they said. They were delighted to assist Lynda in preparing the locks and then to travel on *Frederick* between them. They were so energetically anxious to please that one of them, inevitably, had a nasty bruising spill, but he did not care about the pain in the excitement of actually helping a boat through the flight.

Even with their additional aid, a hire boat pursued us up the flight, catching up with us before the top lock, the crew evidently annoyed at our comparatively slow rate of progress. It seemed that they were 'doing the Cheshire ring' in one week, including 'a nice day's trip up the Caldon'.

For our second night on the canal we tied at a point about halfway along the canal at Endon, just as the countryside was really starting to open up, leaving urbanisation behind. Walking along the path to Hazelhurst junction, we could see the valley dropping below the cut and the distant, beckoning hills of the Peak District.

The damp, overcast weather gave way next morning to sunshine, encouraging us to press on towards Froghall at the top of the canal and reputedly a beauty spot where the river Churnet flowed close to the canal through a mountainous valley. At the junction the route divided, with one arm leading away to the right and then crossing over the aqueduct towards Leek. We continued straight ahead, dropping through the first of three locks.

As Lynda steered *Frederick* into the second lock, I heard the nerve-chilling sound of metal crashing and splintering. I rushed to the boat. Lynda had put the engine in neutral, reporting that indeed there seemed to be some mechanical trouble so that the boat had lost propulsion. Taking over, very carefully, I put the engine in forward gear only to hear a repetition of the dreadful noise of smashing metal, and confirmed that we had lost power.

I walked on down to the bottom lock and found that luckily there was a good place to tie *Frederick*. So, sadly, filled with foreboding about the potential damage, we dragged him down by rope. Once there, I delved again into the weed hatch, but this time there was no offending material. I spent an hour checking every available point – the fuel and electrical connections – but there was nothing visibly wrong. The only conclusion to be drawn was that there had been some kind of break-up within the gear box, since the engine itself was not affected.

Meanwhile, the afternoon had broadened into the finest clear evening that we had experienced yet on the Caldon and the one, small compensation in our troubled state was that our mooring gave us a magnificent view of a glorious sunset over the hills – the destination that we had expected to reach that night.

The rain returned, just a light drizzle at first, on Easter Sunday morning. According to the Ordnance Survey map and guide there should have been a public telephone next to the Holly Bush pub, some 500 yards away; so, wearing our waterproof coats, we set out to try and speak to Malcolm Braine who, it seemed prophetically, had offered to help in such a situation. We thought only of asking him for advice about which local boatbuilder to contact about a problem that appeared to be so serious that we would have to be towed into their yard.

The telephone box was no longer there. It hardly seemed worth returning to *Frederick* to put on our complete rain gear so we walked on to Cheddleton, two miles away, as the weather turned into a downpour. By the time that we found the telephone box above the canal bridge at Cheddleton, our trousers were drenched and water had seeped into our boots so that our feet were sploshing around in them. Although almost every window of the box had been broken, the telephone was working and Malcolm was at home.

'Malcolm, you'll hardly believe this, but *Frederick* has broken down,' I spluttered into the mouthpiece. 'After what you said, only a week ago, as we were leaving Norton Canes, when there was no thought of anything going wrong, can you suggest something?'

The comforting, gentle voice came back: 'Stay where you are and close to the boat. I'll try and contact my engineer, but it is Easter so it may take some time. Call again tomorrow and I hope to have some news.'

Easter Monday morning was bright and sunny. At noon we decided that Lynda would stay on the boat in case someone arrived, while I walked to the Holly Bush to ask if I could use their telephone. Anne behind the bar readily agreed to my using it, and I learned that Malcolm had contacted a fitter and they were expecting to come out later that same day.

Two or three locals in the bare, wood-floored bar – where walkers in heavy boots and thick socks were eating their sandwiches – were full of sympathy for our predicament, including a farmer whose own narrowboat was in dry dock at Stone. A large burly man in a boiler suit, a minute pork-pie hat squashed so firmly on his head that it seemed to be a permanent fixture, offered to use his JCB to lift *Frederick*'s stern out of the water for inspection. I hoped that it would not come to such drastic action. Another kindly offered use of his portable generator.

By late afternoon it seemed unlikely that anyone would come out this far over the bank holiday. We walked back to Cheddleton, this time in better weather, enjoying the lovely valley where the river Churnet bubbled through flood meadows opposite the Leek arm, rising on the hillside among white-washed stone houses and gardens full of spring flowers.

Mrs Braine answered my call. 'Isn't Malcolm with you? He left an hour ago with Terry and they should be there by now.'

We ran all the way back along the two miles to the Holly Bush.

Rounding the last corner, we saw the strange vision of *Frederick* moving along the canal and, just for a moment, it seemed as though he must be working. Then, disappointed, I realised that two men were pulling him along on ropes to bring him to a point outside the pub where they could work more easily.

With considerable ingenuity in the restricted space and gloom of the engine room, Malcolm and Terry managed to separate the propeller shaft from the gearbox, lifting that clear of the engine, already unbolted from the floor and propped on makeshift bearings. The work was accompanied by a Dudley Moore/Peter Cook style of commentary: 'What do you think of that, Terence?' 'Terry, my boy, we've got a little bit of a problem here.' 'Hold on, Terence.' 'What about *this*!' 'Oh, dear, oh dear!' 'My lord!' 'Wow!'

They found that the teeth of the spline connection between the gearbox and propeller shaft had been sheared. 'At least it's not affected the gearbox itself,' were Malcolm's comforting words as he explained that as it was not a standard part they would have to leave the engine in its separated state for a few days while they tried to obtain a replacement.

After they departed in the dark, we had a late, late, very depressed supper.

We settled down to what was inevitably going to be a lengthy wait before *Frederick* would be mobile. First, we had to adopt a disciplined regime over absolutely minimum use of electricity (since the batteries could not be recharged by the engine) and water (since we did not know when we would be able to fill again).

Food supplies were a lesser problem, even though it meant walking again the two miles to Cheddleton where we found that the best shops were situated a further mile from the canal at the top of a steep hill, though at least we could walk downhill carrying the weight. We also discovered one of the finest butchers in the country in a side lane next to the church, and tried to ignore the fact that we had seen animals munching in the backyard alongside his own abattoir.

This time we explored a new route back from the village, climbing higher across the fields behind it until we had distant views of the Peak District towards Buxton, and then stumbling on a path that brought us into an enchanting valley where a stream cascaded down over waterfalls, emerging into a series of lakes where a variety of ducks had made their home. It looked like a reservoir, yet its natural setting of hillsides and trees seemed to discount this. Later we discovered that Deep Hayes nature park had in fact been created imaginatively from a disused reservoir.

Another day, we walked along the Leek arm over the aqueduct, past the stone houses on the canalside – where the gardens, lovingly cared for, displayed early spring flowers – and through a deeply wooded section up to the newly restored tunnel. Climbing over the top, we found that the canal terminated, disappointingly and abruptly, just on the far side of the tunnel; the former connection into the town had been filled in.

On our way back from Leek the rain started again, growing into a deluge. It continued throughout the next day, hammering on the roof, driven by gale-force winds, and we watched, somewhat alarmed, as the river Churnet in the meadow below our mooring breached its banks and rapidly rose until it seemed that it might reach the level of the canal. It gushed, thundering, through the arches of the ancient stone bridge, which we reminded ourselves had survived many previous floods over past centuries.

Opposite, William the bull looked mournfully out of a shed on to the desolate scenery. His depression seemed equal to our own until a telephone call informed us that Terry was returning the next day with the replacement part to restore the engine.

Our optimistic mood did not last long. After refitting all sections, Terry restarted the engine only to find that, unexpectedly, it had become jammed in forward gear. He concluded that the damage must have been more extensive than they had thought, and the gearbox itself would have to be removed for inspection. This time, we decided that before the engine was dismantled we would move *Frederick* to Cheddleton to be closer to the telephone and shops, as well as giving the batteries a charge. We proceeded very slowly and carefully along the canal, since we had no means of stopping quickly or reversing if we encountered any difficulties.

That evening, we treated ourselves to a delicious meal at the Italian restaurant next to the bridge, and the owner readily agreed that we could come alongside and take on water – that problem at least was solved.

Ten days later, after the gearbox had been stripped down and taken to a specialist firm in Stockport for testing, Terry returned to reassemble the engine. This time, there was no unforeseen problem. It functioned. We had a working boat again.

We decided now to return immediately to the Trent and Mersey and push on towards our next target – the Macclesfield canal. We had seen enough of the Caldon, walking the towing-paths. It had been an extraordinarily frustrating three weeks, unfortunately souring our impression of the Caldon. Such a breakdown would have been trying at any time on our travels; it had been especially tiresome occurring so soon after the winter, before we had started to move far.

The experience had made us realise how dependent we were upon a good functioning engine. Without it, we had been more helpless than at any time in the winter and the immobility had made us feel claustrophobic and tense. On the other hand, there had been compensations: we had broken down on a lovely section of canal not far from a telephone and shops, with lots of good walks around.

We had a special bonus one day while we were still immobilised at Cheddleton. A traditonal narrowboat drifted past, almost imperceptibly, water bubbling quietly around its bows, no spluttering engine noise – only the soft, steady plodding of the horse that towed it, pulling on a slender cotton rope 100 feet ahead. The great sturdy shire horse was bedecked attractively with a Victorian-style lace cap and jangling, burnished brasses. The boat moved at least as fast as any craft under power, yet with only the soft sound of water splashing gently around its hull. It made us wonder, in our static state, about the advances achieved by the diesel engine.

Chapter Seven

North to Ellesmere Port

After passing the beautiful bottle-shaped kilns and quiet deserted wharves of former potteries in Stoke – one of the finest sights of industrial archaelogy in Britain – we arrived at the entrance to Harecastle tunnel at 5.30 p.m. and discovered that it was too late in the day to pass through it. In our enthusiasm at being on the move again, I had forgotten to check the instructions: since the tunnel was only wide enough to accommodate a single boat, a keeper at either end regulated the passage of craft.

Although off-duty officially, the keeper told me that we could be the first boat to pass through in the morning. It was no problem; indeed, we were glad to tie in the sheltered cutting leading to the tunnel after travelling for many hours from halfway along the Caldon.

There are, in fact, three tunnels, parallel with each other, under Harecastle hill, just to the north of Stoke-on-Trent. The earliest, designed by James Brindley, was opened in 1777 after eleven years' devastatingly difficult work. At one and three-quarter miles, it was considered the Eighth Wonder of the World, a feat of engineering without equal at that time.

It later became a bottleneck to the fast expanding traffic of the Trent and Mersey, since the singlebeam tunnel had no towing-path and boats had to be legged through it. Thomas Telford was called in to solve the problem and his solution – a second tunnel with a towing-path – was opened in 1822. Each tunnel was operated on a one-way basis until, early in the twentieth century, the original bore had collapsed through mining subsidence to such an extent that it had to be closed. For a further forty years, until 1954, an electric tug was used to speed traffic through Telford's tunnel.

The third tunnel was not built until years after Telford's. It carried the Stoke–Kidsgrove railway, but this in turn was closed some twenty-five years ago when the line was diverted around the hill. This means that there is only one of the set of three still in use, now the third longest on British waterways and only some 100 yards shorter than Blisworth, though a much smaller bore. The modern entrance is, curiously, through the square brick walls of an overhead office building, thus disguising the original semi-circle of the tunnel, and boats have to pass under a hanging gantry to check that they are sufficiently low.

The next morning, *Frederick*'s bow was already immersed in the tunnel when I put the engine in reverse to correct our alignment. The engine did not respond; it simply revved as though in neutral. I found that, as at Hazelhurst, there was no longer any propulsion, although this time there was no noise of smashing metal.

I had had a niggling suspicion as we came through Stoke that the engine was not performing correctly; now my immediate reaction was that this was a repeated failure of the gearbox. Lynda on the bow was already into the tunnel as I shouted out: 'We've broken down again!'

In total disbelief that this could be happening to us, we pulled *Frederick* back by rope to our overnight mooring. Explaining to the keeper that we had only just recovered from a serious mechanical breakdown, he was most sympathetic and offered use of his telephone; but first I delved once again into the engine room.

While other boats were arriving and passing into the tunnel, I made a careful check of all parts and found what seemed to be the cause, although at that stage I could not be certain that it was the only failure. It appeared that bolts on the connection plate between the gearbox and the propeller shaft had become detached. Searching around the bilge, I found some bolts and nuts, reassembled them, and we were under way again.

It was not a comforting start to travelling through Harecastle tunnel, the most daunting on the British waterways. Just after passing for the second time under the height-measuring device, doors behind were slammed shut, sealing off the daylight, and a fume-extraction fan was switched on, ear-splitting noise echoing through the eerie, vast blackness of the shaft. Notices had warned that the towing-path to the right was incomplete, and after a few hundred yards it disappeared; there was thus no guidance to potential underwater hazards. I steered the boat as close to the left side as possible. Above, the roughly hewn rock surface descended at places so low that *Frederick*'s roof barely skimmed beneath it and I had to crouch on the counter, only just able to peer ahead.

After an interminable time of total blackness, the first greyness of the Kidsgrove end started to take shape and there was never a more welcome sight than the growing half-moon glow of daylight at the far end. *Frederick* emerged like a chrysalis breaking out of its hard shell.

A short way beyond, a sharp left turn took *Frederick* on to the arm of the Macclesfield canal which crossed on an aqueduct back over the Trent and Mersey. At this point, though still much concerned about the state of the engine, we felt a great surge of relief at reaching the next target of the year: a canal that had seemed as though it might be bewitched after we had seen Macclesfield-based narrowboats called *Sorceress* and *Evil O*.

There was something enchanted about the start of the canal. It was dominated by a strange, awesome hill that rose starkly from flattish countryside to a craggy point, capped by the outline of a ruined castle. It had the extraordinary name of Mow Cop. We felt a hypnotic urge to climb and explore it.

We tied at the foot of the hill at Kent Green, a small village of many pubs, and waited in the Rising Sun for John and Penny's arrival from London for the weekend. Sitting next to us in the bar, a local man described his daily routine of circuiting the range of hostelries, always starting at the Bird in Hand, a genuine traditional house where real ale was brought to the bare wooden bar in a jug from casks in the cellar.

'Can you walk up to Mow Cop from here?' we asked.

'Yes, indeed, you can,' he replied firmly. 'Several summers ago I did it. Yes, I remember starting from the Three Horseshoes and climbing part of the way before stopping for brief refreshment at the Cheshire View, then continuing on to the Globe and the Ash. On my way, I also found that there were good breaks at the Crown and the Mow Cop. Now this was Sunday, mind you, when it's supposed that pubs close at two o'clock, but just as I was leaving the last one in mid-afternoon, our local bobby happened to come by and he thought that I needed a lift back down here. So, I suppose it's true that I walked only to the top, not down again.'

'Now, what I suggest you ought to do is to take a look at the woods around here,' he ruminated. 'There's many a lovely local lady that I've taken to show her our woods, and a piece more no doubt. Anyways, I must be off now – my wife's waiting for me to bring our supper back from the local chippy.'

The next morning was bright and clear, though *Frederick* was being buffeted by a bitter gale-force wind. We walked with John and Penny along the towing-path to Ramsdell Hall, a fine redbrick mansion, set on immaculate lawns and a brilliant yellow carpet of daffodils. Opposite, a mile away, we could see the National Trust property of Little Moreton Hall, regarded as a supreme example of the black and white timbered style.

With the fierce wind behind us, we climbed steeply through meadows and woods towards the peak of Mow Cop, and finally up the jagged rocky summit to the castle. It turned out to be a fake. The round tower and castellated walls were 'demolished by an unknown battle before they were completed'. What did occur at this place on 31 May 1822 was the first meeting of the Primitive Methodists. A plaque commemorating the event records that it was organised by William Clowes and lasted for fourteen hours. Even today, when modern houses have been built below the crag, it is a remote spot; in the early nineteenth century, it must have been wild and desolate. Why was this place chosen for the meeting? It seemed a more likely choice for a witches' sabbath or an orgy. The Macclesfield canal was living up to our expectations.

On the top of the tower, the wind was so powerful that it threw

Penny and me off balance, but the view in this clear weather was magnificent. Looking west across the great green patchwork of the Cheshire plain, we could discern the white saucers of Jodrell Bank and, behind, the massive blueish line of the Welsh mountains. On the northern horizon there was a glint of silver through a pall of smoke, perhaps the Mersey at Ellesmere Port, our next destination. A clump of hills to the south and, inland, the deep valleys of the Caldon beyond the sprawling mass of Stoke.

When we stopped for a well deserved rest in the Cheshire View, a local reckoned that the wind was colder than at any time in the winter. There were a few flurries of snow.

Over the next ten miles from Kent Green to Bosley flight, the line of hills rising steeply to the right of the canal were enrobed in a soft, swirling mist that cast mystifying, haunting shadows around the crevices.

After Congleton the canal rose above the dimly visible Cheshire plain on the left, carried on a straight embankment, one of the features of this canal. The waterway passed over the deep valley of the river Dane on a perfectly proportioned stone aqueduct and arrived at the bottom of the only flight of locks on the Macclesfield.

The fairly direct line of the Macclesfield, with its concentration of locks within a single flight, ideally illustrated the development of engineering skills and design which had taken place in only some fifty years since the opening of the Caldon in 1779. The Caldon was one of the last works of James Brindley, regarded as the founder of the English canals, and the Macclesfield was one of the late designs of Thomas Telford, who was mainly responsible for completing the system. Although others, such as Jessop, Smeaton and Rennie, were much involved in detailed planning and execution, most of the development of England's canals in the extraordinarily rapid space of about seventy years was due to Brindley and Telford.

Neither of the two men had the kind of learning and training which would be expected of any civil engineer undertaking quite modest schemes in the twentieth century. Both were largely self-taught, learning through daring experiment, many trials and tribulations, yet pioneering immeasurable advances in engineering design and leaving an immense mark on the British landscape.

Brindley started work in a flintmill at Leek, similar to one which had been restored to full working order where we tied at Cheddle-ton. It sounds a humble background, yet in the eighteenth century water- and windmills were considered the height of technology, providing power for early industrial production. It so happened that Brindley was engaged on a complex scheme for mine drainage at the time that the Duke of Bridgewater became interested in the concept of carrying coal by boat from his mines, and Brindley's skills were drawn into the project. Once involved, he was caught in the fever of providing urgently needed water transport throughout the country and he devoted the last thirteen years of his life to the routes which would link the Thames with the Mersey and the Severn with the Trent, known as The Cross.

There was little previous experience in England to guide Brindley in bringing water uphill against its natural tendency to course down to the sea. Although the coast-to-coast Canal du Midi had been built in France some ninety years earlier, Brindley was only partially literate and used his natural instincts in planning a canal route by following a chosen contour, keeping rigidly to the lines of the hillside, usually close to the stream of a river which supplied water, until obstacles were met that could be passed only by a tunnel or cutting.

So Brindley's style has survived in the winding, sometimes tortuous line of canals such as the Staffs and Worcs and the Oxford. Josiah Wedgwood, who became his most important patron by seizing the opportunity to transport his ceramics by water, commented: 'I am afraid he will do too much, and leave us before his vast designs are executed; he is so incessantly harassed on every side, that he hath no rest, either for his mind, or body.' His prediction was fulfilled when Brindley died in 1772 after becoming drenched while surveying the Caldon and failing to take proper care of himself.

Telford was born in the Lowlands of Scotland in 1757, at about the time that Brindley first became involved in the Bridgewater canal. Serving an apprenticeship as a stonemason, he was fortunate in having a wealthy local employer who encouraged him to take an adventurous interest in building design, and quite soon Telford went to London to work with Robert Adam in the construction of Somerset House.

He was assiduously devoted to self-education throughout his life, spending all his (not very many) spare hours extending his reading and knowledge. His great break came in 1787 when he was appointed as Shropshire's surveyor and made his mark in enormously improving the roads and bridges leading to north Wales. He also inherited the problems of the over-ambitious projected canal link between Llangollen and Chester; he solved them by constructing the Pontcysyllte aqueduct, carrying the canal in an iron trough more than 1,000 feet over the river Dee at a height of 120 feet. It was built, against all odds, in 1805 and there has been nothing since then to equal it in Britain.

With some thirty years of previous canal-building experience to draw upon, Telford was able to improve on Brindley's rather simplistic approach and tried to achieve a more economic, time-saving and direct route by constructing embankments and bridges. Even so, like Brindley, he became exhausted by the endless demands on his time and his health collapsed under the strain of trying to sort out the near-failure of the high embanked line at Nantwich. Before he died in 1834, Telford had laid the foundations of a new profession by founding up the Institute of Civil Engineers.

At Bosley, Telford created one of the most scenically beautiful flights in England. Approached along an embankment and aqueduct, twelve stone locks are spaced at regular intervals, almost in a straight line, set among sheep pastures – totally rural and peaceful. Each lock, gradually lifting the boat 118 feet to the summit, opens up a still more splendid view of the Cloud, whose slopes ascend gently and steadily through a patchwork of fields to open moorland near the peak.

Our next port of call was to be Macclesfield itself. We had to make two business visits to London separated by a week, so that the town's connection with the Euston–Manchester InterCity line was ideal. Between the two trips, we thought there would be time to make a return cruise to Marple at the head of the canal.

As the hills closed in, dramatically, becoming steeper and sheerer, it was difficult to visualise how the canal could find a passage to Macclesfield. Then, passing through a rocky cutting, we arrived on the edge of the town and discovered that the railway station was about a mile away. Beyond it, we climbed up a cobbled street that burst the lungs and strained the legs, and found a thriving regional centre around dignified, elegant public buildings. There was a reward at the top of the steep street at a baker's shop which sold northern oat cakes (like flat cold pancakes) and potato cakes. Further on, the excellent range of shops included a street of tantalising boutiques into which Lynda plunged with enthusiasm. Her birthday was not far away, so I was delighted to find more than one possibility for a present.

The next day's journey on the InterCity service to London was uneventful; unlike many past experiences on the Birmingham line, there was ample room and no fighting for the last seat. We were worried, however, about our return, since this was to be on a Friday when we found that Euston is usually swamped with a mass exodus of weekenders – somehow, we always seemed to have to return from London visits on Friday nights! This time, on arriving in London, I had the foresight to reserve seats.

True to our expectations, Euston concourse at 7 p.m. on Friday was engulfed by a mass of people, snaking queues tangling with one another so that it was almost impossible to identify the right one for any particular platform. Glancing at the departure board, I noticed that not only was the 7.35 p.m. to Manchester via Macclesfield announced, but there was also another train departing fifteen minutes earlier.

Encouraged by an amiable man in the queue, we picked up our bags, rushed through the barrier and clambered aboard just as the train was leaving. We looked around to find that, though it was crowded, there were still spare seats. Then we realised that the carriage was of the kind of post-war rolling-stock that had been phased out of normal operation years ago. Moreover, there was no refreshment car of any description on the train.

Despite our growing doubts, the train took off along the line at breakneck speed, the orange sodium lights of London left behind as the ancient carriages seemed to leap from the track. Its passengers shaken and pounded, swung and crashed from side to side, the train rattled madly along as though determined to prove, like an elderly jogger, that it suffered from no deterioration of age. Then it gave a last gasp, exhausted, and almost without any perceptible slowing-down, halted.

All movement ceased abruptly. No longer was there any sound of the heaving engine. All was silence. The BR staff had disappeared as quickly as the train halted. We were isolated on a distant siding within sight of Rugby station, yet separated by intervening lines. The train slumped in this place for nearly two hours; announcements echoing from the station appeared to have no relevance to our predicament, while other trains – including no doubt the 7.35 p.m. InterCity to Manchester via Macclesfield on which we had reserved seats – roared past without stopping.

On this forgotten ghost train, the pent-up fury of frustrated passengers exploded as some of them started to shout abuse at the one lonely porter on the dimly lit platform. At last, another engine jolted on to our line of carriages and we moved away at a sedate pace, eventually reaching Macclesfield more than four hours after leaving Euston, twice the scheduled time. We realised we had made the mistake, that we swore we would not repeat, of joining one of the special unscheduled relief services provided to transport the great weekend crowd away from London.

The next day we returned with immense relief to travelling at our own pace on *Frederick*. We pushed along the shallow canal through Bollington, where deserted granite textile mills, several storeys high, looked as grand as the hotels of Harrogate, and continued on another section of high embankment. The penalty for today's boater of Telford's practice of grouping locks into flights was, we discovered, that the single concentrated flight of locks at Bosley had produced such silted conditions that there were few places on the Macclesfield where it was possible to divert from the middle channel. Two centuries later, there was something after all to be said for Brindley's system of locks spread out more spaciously.

Telford's bridges, however, were an endless delight to the eye with their symmetrical perfection. Nearly a hundred of them over twenty-eight miles, sometimes so awkwardly angled over the canal's route that they were difficult to navigate, yet each one individually, beautifully designed, constructed from blocks of stone separately carved to conform with the shape of the bridge arch, hewn by craftsmen who in earlier generations might have been building cathedrals. Extra distinction had been added in recent years by the local canal society, which had placed attractive cast-iron number-plates on them.

At Marple, the highest point on the connected English waterways, we admired a pair of beautifully constructed, perfectly proportioned roving bridges that snaked across the canal, originally giving unimpeded passage to the horse so that its line could be carried without interruption from one side to the other.

We arrived, beyond the second of the roving bridges, at the junction with the Peak Forest canal, now a vital link on the route to Manchester and thereby connecting with the Shropshire Union. It was not always so: there was a twelve-year period from 1962 when navigation was abandoned, but the canal was subsequently restored by the combined efforts of the Peak Forest canal society, IWA and BWB. It was one of the great success stories of recent waterways regeneration.

For once, our scheduled return to Macclesfield and thence to London meant that we had no time to explore further by boat, so we walked down the flight of sixteen locks, which dropped the canal 218 feet over one mile. It passed through a parkland of high beeches, clinging to the steep hillsides, and arrived on an aqueduct poised above the deep valley of the river Goyt, flowing fast over a multitude of small, noisy waterfalls. On this day, at last, the spring sunshine seemed to be taking on the warmth of summer, and the river glinted brightly through branches whose nakedness was just covered with filmy green leaves. At the root of the trees, the pubescent shoots of bluebells were starting to shaft through the earth. Mating birds called sharply, urgently from one side of the valley to the other, seeking for their partners. It had been a late, cold spring; now there was a feeling that life and growth were responding to the sudden urge of the warm day.

In the second week of May, winter seemed to have returned with a vengeance, bringing bitingly cold winds and days of continuous torrential rain, culminating in a thunderstorm at Middlewich when we were worried that lightning would strike the boat.

We travelled along the section of the Trent and Mersey between Church Lawton and Hassall Green known as 'heartbreak hill' because the locks are frequent, yet spaced out so that, unlike in a flight, each one is just too far away to be prepared in advance of the on-coming boat. Once again, the narrowbeam locks were different from any we had previously encountered: arranged in pairs so that, ideally, there should have been a chance that one or other was in favour of a boat either ascending or descending. Theoretically, it would seem to be the perfect lock system, efficient and water-saving, better suited to today's needs than widebeam locks. In practice, it did not work out like that since several locks were out of order, thus spoiling any possible operating sequence.

At Thurlwood we saw one of the most curious locks on the entire system. Contained within a massive, complicated steel cage, it was built in 1957 to overcome the subsidence so prevalent in this area from salt-mining. It was not successful, so was no longer in use.

The connecting arm from Middlewich brought us to the Shropshire Union at Barbridge and we returned to widebeam locks for the rest of the journey to Ellesmere Port. When, a few weeks later, we came back and this time continued on to Nantwich and the junction at Autherley with the Staffs and Worcs, we found that the locks through this southern part of the Shroppie were narrowbeam. Such changes can be confusing to today's boater.

The explanation lies in the muddled history of what is now known, rather grandly, as the Shropshire Union, and provides one of the great cross-country routes, linking the Mersey with the Severn. It started life in a far humbler way in 1772 as the Chester canal, conceived as a means of restoring the prosperity of the port of Chester on the river Dee by providing a link to Nantwich which by-passed the threatening competition of the Trent and Mersey. Twenty years later, the line was extended across the neck of Wirral to provide a direct outlet to the Mersey at a place then called Whitby as part of an ambitious scheme to link up with the canals, already partially built, which started in the Welsh mountains at Llangollen and Montgomery. There were many vacillations before the connection was finally made via the Shropshire town of Ellesmere, and thus the interchange point on the Mersey was renamed Ellesmere Port.

It seems extraordinary that it was not until 1835 – at a time when the railways were already dissecting the country – that an entirely different company, the Birmingham and Liverpool Junction, completed the natural, economically important link between Nantwich and Autherley, thus opening up the burgeoning markets of the West Midlands as well as providing a through route down the Staffs and Worcs to the Severn and Bristol. Ten years later, the two separate companies merged to form the Shropshire Union.

Ten days after setting out from Marple, we again had a day when the sun was warm, hot enough to be wearing shorts. The wide canal gently curved, at places almost like a river, through fields so lush that the cattle were wading through deep green grass. In this richest of dairy countryside, imposing red sandstone farms were set in expansive fields, dotted like dominoes with black and white cows, abundant in milk.

In other fields new-born lambs leapt spontaneously, kicking their hind legs with the sheer joy of being alive. The canal banks were coloured with variegated spring flowers: thick bunches of cowslips, a brighter shade of pale yellow, contrasted with the pure white stars of flax; in the wet spots the deeper, more luxuriant yellow of kingcups and the iridescent purple of bluebells. At Bate's Mill trees around the lock were decked with foamy blossom, while steep gardens were ablaze with daffodil trumpets.

At Bunbury, we reached the first pair, a staircase, of locks on the Shroppie. Still legible in peeling paint on the side of the old brick warehouse was the historic title 'Shropshire Union Railway and Canal Company'.

There was a further significance to Bunbury. Was this the place, I wondered, that Algernon in *The Importance of Being Earnest* (which we had seen at Leamington during the winter) had identified as his rural escape away from London sophistication? Did this name inspire Oscar Wilde to invent the word 'Bunburying' to describe the unconventional behaviour of someone like Algernon who wished 'to go down to the country whenever I choose'? Is there any evidence that Oscar Wilde himself used to steal away from the tittle-tattle of city gossip to enjoy the different scene of Bunbury which, in his day, would have been thriving with working boats, a changeover stabling point for horses? On the other hand, it may have been a name picked with a pin from the map, or even created from his imagination. As he remarks elsewhere in the play, 'The truth is rarely pure, never simple.'

Coming from the lower of the two locks, Bunbury took on a different significance for us when, once again, the propulsion failed. It was the third such incident since entering Harecastle tunnel and, being simple to repair, it had ceased to be a worry and was just a nuisance. Meanwhile, in London, I had talked with my brother who has great experience of building sea-going motor yachts. Acting on his advice, I went through a systematic procedure of tightening the bolts on the connection between the propeller shaft and gearbox as though fixing a car wheel. Using a plastic credit card to measure the gap, each nut was turned in rotation until a perfect balance had been obtained. It was the last time that we had this problem.

Beyond here, at Beeston, there was a dramatic change in the landscape. A series of small rocky hills erupted from the flat plain: one crowned by a derelict castle, the other by the romantic fairy-tale turrets of Peckforton, Lord Tollemache's mansion. It seemed as though the Rhineland had come to Shropshire.

We tied on a popular spot near the canalside Shady Oak pub – and together with my son Simon and Patricia, who had joined us for the weekend – walked across fields to the sheer face of Beeston Castle and made the steep ascent to the top.

Built in the thirteenth century by Sir Ranulff and his heirs, who became the earls of Chester, it played an important role for the Tudors in policing the Welsh borders, though it really came into its own during the exciting times of the Civil War. Then it changed hands three times between the Royalists and Parliamentarians. On one occasion, this seemingly impregnable fortress was infiltrated after dark by a Royalist captain – who must have been a forerunner of our contemporary SAS – and his band of ten commandos. He sat and enjoyed dinner with the Roundhead commander, who capitulated the next morning, reported back to his own headquarters and was promptly executed. Life was a little more harsh in those days.

Our climb was rewarded with fabulous views – Mow Cop now at one extremity, Ellesmere Port at the other. It was the sort of viewing point that encourages people to become pedantically boring in identifying places they recognise.

'Look, there's the bend in the road we drove along, there, d'you see it?'

'Yes, but that patch of green, if you follow the bend for another 500 yards, isn't that where we had our picnic lunch?'

'Maybe, but look, for certain, that redbrick building by the cross-roads, that must be where we stopped for a drink at the pub.'

We returned to *Frederick* and sat outside; it was a clear evening and the shadows cast by the sunset exaggerated the castle's scale. In a meadow below the canal, a herd of cows moved across a small stream separating one side of the field from the other. Most of the cattle waded through the muddy waters, yet there was one that held back, hovered uncertainly, then trotted positively towards a plank bridge that crossed the stream 100 yards away. Keeping her feet dry, she passed over and joined the rest of the herd. One or two butted her playfully as if to say, 'Didn't you want to get your feet wet?'

As we drew closer to Chester, I started to expound on my knowledge of the city. In earlier years, it had been a cultural haven when I had spent winter weeks square-bashing on Wirral as a raw National Service recruit and, later, trained as a journalist with the *Liverpool Daily Post and Echo*. 'It's a lovely city,' I remarked to Lynda, 'but it's not going to be so interesting to me as other places since I know it so well.'

I was wrong. Chester came as a revelation to me for several reasons, two in particular. Firstly, there had been considerable change, as in so many other regional centres, over the past twenty years or so. Secondly, I had not seen it before from the different perspective of the canal.

Modern development had been handled well in Chester: the street layout had been retained, new buildings erected behind existing frontages, and much of the passing traffic removed so that it was more possible than ever before to appreciate the picturesque black and white two-tiered shopping arcades of the Rows jutting and leaning at odd angles. Enhanced by brilliant sunshine, crowds of tourists in light, colourful summer wear milled around the pedestrian precinct, Italian in their gaiety. The bell-ringing of the Dickensian town-crier, publicising tourist attractions, gave a theatrical touch.

It was reassuring to find dimly recollected, once familiar sights: the imposing Victorian gothic town hall, the ornate gilded clock on the Eastgate bridge over the main road, and the deep warm shadows within the red sandstone cathedral. A *new* discovery was that the canal ran close to these points that I had known well in the past. Cut under the rock base of the city walls, it dropped through an awe-inspiring three-lock staircase into a basin from which further locks led on to the river Dee and the former port. It was a secret world that I had not known existed, yet it lay immediately below the busy roads circuiting the city centre.

Two or three minutes' walk from our mooring we found steps up to the medieval walls that completely encircle the city, and from there we strolled, detached and unaffected by the traffic in the streets below, to a corner tower giving fabulous views over the broad river. We clambered down steep steps, twisting among houses built into the rock-face, and wandered along the fine waterfront.

Although I had thought that I knew Chester quite well, it is a city of hidden places, with few dramatic vistas. The walls tightly enclosed and preserved the historic town, preventing radical change, so that layer upon layer of building has been raised above the original Roman foundations, here and there exposed to view. In a few days, we felt that we had insufficient time to seek out and uncover the wealth of potential interest in Chester.

Lynda celebrated her birthday during our stay in Chester and her Taurean star must have been under an adverse influence at the time. In contrast to the previous day, it started with torrential rain that settled down to a soupy drizzle, and we set about stocking up in preparation for our departure to Ellesmere Port. We needed a new cylinder of propane gas and several sacks of solid fuel, and I managed to track down by telephone suppliers who agreed to deliver to our mooring alongside a service road. While I stayed on board to look after these deliveries, Lynda trudged off in the wet to buy groceries from the new Tesco supermarket on the other side of the road, though she found this was only a back entrance, locked for security, and had to wheel a laden trolley around the block.

Meanwhile, in search of some engine parts, I had come across a launderette half a mile away. At this time, our on-board generator had developed a fault so that we could not use the washing-machine. I conducted Lynda to the launderette, returning to *Frederick* for the second phase of deliveries.

After slaving throughout her birthday, I suggested that we should go in the evening to a smart Chinese restaurant attractively situated above the canal, just the right place for Lynda to wear for the first time the brilliant green silk jumpsuit that I had bought in Macclesfield – her birthday present. It was damp, though no longer raining, as we walked 100 yards to the restaurant where the lighting was as romantically dim as a night-club. I ordered a bottle of champagne. The waiter exploded the cork, poured foaming glasses, stumbled and sent a glass and part of the bottle all over Lynda's brand new outfit.

The manager rose to the occasion when I explained exactly what had happened. The delicious meal was 'on the house' and we felt able to indulge in another bottle of champagne.

Arriving, the next morning, at the top of the staircase locks, the keeper told us that no boats could pass through for the next thirty minutes: there was a diver at work in the bottom lock.

A group of people were gathered around it, peering over the side. There was no sign of the diver in the murky water until we followed the line of an air pipe to bubbles rising to the surface. Shortly, a helmet appeared and a gloved hand waved in the air a milk-crate, followed by other assorted objects which had been blocking the gates.

By now, Chester's horse-drawn tourist boat had arrived below the flight, while a short narrowboat had joined *Frederick* at the top. Everyone started to move forward into the widebeam locks at the same time, both top and bottom. The situation contained the elements of potential catastrophe in which the three boats would meet in the middle lock, like a London traffic jam in which no one would give way, everyone tooting on horns.

Calmness prevailed. The tourist boat, so well experienced, took charge. As *Frederick* dropped from the top into the middle lock, there was ample space to pass the ascending full-length tourist boat and then for the shorter boat to push across. There was no need for any hooting; the operation was carried out rationally and quietly, the two sets of boats passing in their opposite directions.

Shortly afterwards, we reached the outskirts of Chester and approached a point where the canal narrowed. Two young boys were crouched on the side; although it was not sun-bathing weather, they appeared to be naked as cherubs in a Rubens painting. As *Frederick* nudged past the point, both opened their legs, one displaying cheekily his pre-pubescent parts, the other, more coyly, screening them with a few leaves of plants.

'What are you going to be when you grow up?' asked Lynda. 'A flasher?'

Ellesmere Port kept itself hidden until we reached it. It was totally screened by the vast industrial complex of Stanlow oil refinery, rows upon rows of high round containers, great blocks of faceless buildings, thin metallic chimneys emitting bright orange flames as though drawn from the earth's core, a place with few signs of human life, cut off from the canal by barbed-wire fences, surrounded by an area of industrial dereliction.

After leaving Chester we had passed through the pleasant rolling countryside of Wirral – Liverpool's Surrey – and I began to wonder why we had come this far. Rather vaguely, I knew of the Boat Museum. I had read about the recent restoration of Telford's warehouses, once set alight by hooligans. Even so, we had not had much interest in the static record of museums when on the waterways we could experience the living world.

We discovered that Ellesmere Port is an enchanting, enthralling place, truly a living museum. It is not one building, as I had imagined, but many. Nor is it one basin, but three linked by locks descending from the inland canals to the wide Manchester Ship Canal, itself abutting the expanse of the Mersey. And it is not really a museum, in the sense that the port is still an integral part of the waterways system, boats passing through it *en route* to the Bridge-water canal, Manchester and Marple.

Ellesmere is better endowed, offering much more of interest to the sightseer than the better known St Katharine's Dock next to the Tower of London. The elegantly designed, ruby brick buildings of every shape and size are placed attractively around the three basins descending to the level of the Mersey. The large warehouses have been converted to display centres where the history of the waterways is recreated graphically; smaller workshops and cottages have been returned to their original functions. The wharves are lined with selected examples of different craft from skeletal wooden barges to coasters that carried, until not long ago, chemical products.

We were sitting in the boatman's cabin – admiring the beautiful fittings designed to make use of every part of the small space – of *Gifford*, a former Fellows, Morton and Clayton working boat, when Andy Millward looked through the hatch, helpfully asking if we needed any explanation. We went to see his own former FMC boat, *Monarch*, half converted and moored alongside other fine craft in the middle basin.

He was one of the original group of enthusiasts with sufficient foresight to start trying to save Ellesmere Port at a time when its future was uncertain. They were struggling to raise money by voluntary effort and planning a gradual restoration over many years when Michael Heseltine, then Environment Secretary, arrived on the scene in the wake of the Merseyside rioting. 'How much do you need to put this place back in order?' he enquired.

The committee was given some twenty-four hours to decide on a budget. 'Three and a half million pounds,' was their estimate, a sum which seemed wildly beyond their dreams. The grant was awarded, and since then further government aid has been put into this worthwhile effort to recreate life in the midst of a run-down, depressed area.

Frederick was tied above the lock to the first basin. From here, we looked out on the gleaming waters of the Mersey, just perceiving through dusky, polluted gloom the distant shape of the twin towers of Liverpool's famous Cunard building at the pierhead, a monument to past wealth created through Atlantic and international shipping trade.

This year, we knew that we were unlikely to travel any further north, even though there were waterways beyond our sight, crossing the Pennines from Leeds to Liverpool. Now we had to turn back south, along the Shroppie and down the Severn towards the most westerly point of the system.

Andy came on board *Frederick* and we talked of our plans. 'Do you know about the lock into Gloucester docks?' he asked. 'No? Then let me warn you about it – it's the trickiest place I've come across. You approach down a narrow, fast-flowing side stream of the river which runs over an unprotected weir immediately to the right of the lock. If the gates are closed, it's really difficult and dangerous as there's a high stone wall with few ladders – somehow, I managed to make a flying leap on to a ladder, and just caught the rope around a stanchion in time to hold the boat, which was already being swept along by the current. I can tell you, it was hair-raising.'

His words stayed in our minds as we set out, southwards, towards Stourport where the Staffs and Worcs inter-connects with the Severn.

Chapter Eight

Retreat from the Severn

Stourport should never have been built. It became the terminus of the Staffordshire and Worcestershire canal only after the local people objected to James Brindley's original choice of Bewdley – a natural selection since Bewdley was an established shipping port on the river Severn with a fine waterfront of quays and wharves to prove it.

The hamlet of Lower Mitton, where the river Stour joined the Severn, was therefore designated as the interconnection between the canal, bringing manufactured goods on narrowboats from the Midlands, and the Severn. Here goods were transferred on to Severn sailing trows for shipment to Gloucester and Bristol, thence around the world. So Stourport, as it was renamed, became perhaps the first New Town to be planned for industrial and transportation reasons, some two centuries in advance of the twentieth-century planners' dreams of Milton Keynes, Stevenage, Harlow and Corby.

We first learned of Bewdley, and its habit of rejecting navigation improvements, on arriving in the centre of Kidderminster under the great tower of the parish church and the beckoning hand of a life-sized statue of Richard Baxter, the seventeenth-century philosopher who advocated 'unity and comprehension' in religion. A twentieth-century publican had seized the opportunity to promote his modern hostelry by inviting boaters to follow the direction in which the hand was pointing.

Passing through the lock on our way down the Staffs and Worcs towards Stourport, many other boats were returning, battered and bewildered by their experiences over a bank holiday rally at Bewdley. Some thirty assorted craft, many narrowboats unsuited to the rough conditions, had ventured upstream beyond the Severn's present limit of navigation to demonstrate at Bewdley their support for a new project to revive the ancient right of navigation. Sadly, they told us how they had been greeted at Bewdley with abuse, rotten eggs and other unpleasant missiles.

The rally had been carried out in adverse weather conditions with the best of intentions. The river was officially closed to boating, being in a state of flood, but the convoy had decided to risk the conditions to demonstrate the potential offered by the higher Severn for leisure use.

'It was a bit hairy,' one of them told me, 'but the flood level actually helped us to cross the main obstacle to upstream navigation: an underwater bar about halfway between Stourport and Bewdley. It's said that this was the isolated point at which the old boatmen used to throw off some of the coal they were carrying from north Wales, after they had been weighed, to lighten their load and make the job easier.'

The Severn has had a curious history as a navigation. Evidence supports the claim that at one time it was among the most heavily used waterways in Europe, certainly in Britain. Yet river control was never improved beyond the elementary flash-lock system – though Telford made plans for introducing pound locks – so that commercial transport deserted the river some 200 years ago in favour of the more advanced Midlands canal outlets.

Nevertheless, the rights of navigation through to Welshpool cannot be questioned. A recent study by highly qualified lawyers, published by the Sports Council, affirmed that Parliamentary statutes and historic record placed the navigation rights of the Severn beyond any doubt.

A tourist leaflet published by the Town Clerk of Bewdley, no less, confirms this historic situation:

> The town of Bewdley is situated on the edge of the Wyre Forest and alongside the river Severn. Five hundred years ago, more goods were moved on that river than on any other British waterway and Bewdley became one of the busiest inland ports. With the coming of the canals and, later, the railways, Bewdley's trade ebbed away and most of its earlier importance was lost.

The Higher Severn Navigation Trust has recently put forward practicable plans to restore this boating affluence – though of course now for leisure and tourism use – and their survey, conducted by a leading firm of civil engineers, closely coincides with Telford's original conception for the siting of locks and weirs.

The scheme, if carried out, would provide navigation once again right up to Welshpool, the original source of mineral-carrying transport down the Severn. Boaters on their journey would pass under Andrew Darby's great Ironbridge, which has become a major tourist attraction in the New Town named after Telford. Yet even here, reputedly, the local authority has been indifferent, at best, about the overall concept of restoring a once famous and prosperous navigation. At Bewdley, local inhabitants remain as dogmatically entrenched against any new development as they were when by-passed two centuries ago.

We had travelled from Ellesmere Port to Stourport – both places specially constructed for canal transhipment – during the last days of May and the first week of June, traditionally recognised as one of the most dry and sunny periods of the British summer. The weather had been turbulent with unceasing high winds and periods of torrential rain.

On a day of gale-force winds on the Shropshire Union, we had been held up in approaching a lock by the uncertain behaviour of two full-length narrowboats. They had wavered from side to side, one of them ending up on the non-towing-path side of the entrance, apparently in great difficulty. From some distance behind, I tried to keep control of *Frederick*, edging it along at the slowest pace against the wind, wondering what was happening. It appeared that the boats were crewed entirely by nubile young neophytes, dressed in pure white garments blowing wildly in the wind.

Finally, after ascending the lock, in the straight and shallow cut beyond it, we caught up with one of the boats, by now firmly grounded on the side, driven into the mud by the wind. Several of them were trying to push off the boat, thrusting hard on shafts from the roof, bow and stern.

As we approached, desperately trying to keep *Frederick* on a straight course against the pressure of the vicious wind, some of the young women looked appealingly towards me and cried out for help. Recalling the fate of Orpheus in the deadly waters of the Styx, I could not afford to look back at them. I could hear their frantic cries: 'Help! Help! Can you give us a tow?' The wind blew away my answer: 'If I stop for a second, I'll be cast on to one side and make the situation worse!'

Two hours later, after we had paused for lunch in the shelter of Market Drayton, the boats arrived, and I discovered that the beautiful sirens came from Australia. Soon they were surrounded by the lusty youths who should have been positioned to help them a few miles back along the canal.

The wind was blowing, just as fiercely, on our arrival into the upper basin of Stourport. Leaving Lynda on the boat in the bottom canal lock, I walked ahead to search out a mooring among the congestion of narrowboats and sea-going cruisers that were tied end-on to the quay. The resident lockkeeper explained that I would have to find a place next to the new information centre and water point immediately below the lock.

Taking over the steering, I decided, rather recklessly, to position *Frederick*'s stern on to the side since that way it was easier to climb on and off. I had not judged the strength of the wind accurately, however. It caught the sides of the boat every-which-way. I lost control. A woman appeared from one of the other moored boats and shouted for the stern rope so that she could pull *Frederick* into place. I threw the line and she pulled with all her might, but it was not enough; *Frederick* started to drift dangerously across the line of boats.

Judging that there was no hope of entering the mooring in this uncontrolled way, I started the engine to reverse out of the situation and instantaneously realised that the stern line was hanging in the water. Too late! I saw it dragged by the propeller, even as I cut the engine, under the stern. There could be no doubt that it had become wound around the shaft.

This was the most embarrassing situation for any skipper. The boat was being thrown by the wind against a line of other craft and I could not use our engine power to move away. We were out of control.

Fortunately, we managed to hitch on to another boat's stern and stabilise our position while I descended, once again, into the engine room, unbolted the weed-hatch cover, and began the lengthy process of feeling in the cold water, inch by inch, how to unwind our line. At least, on this occasion, I knew the cause of the trouble.

As I tussled with the rope, I prayed that the boat was safely tied above; I stripped off my shirt and changed into a pair of shorts since the work was so hot and exhausting. Then, some thirty minutes later, dripping from my underwater investigations, I emerged triumphant: I had managed to unravel the rope without the need to cut it.

We moored, this time, bow on to the quay, and went to explore Stourport. Two upper basins were separated by a simple brick Victorian warehouse surmounted by an elegant white cupola clock-tower; they were full of a mixture of canal and sea-going boats. Below, there were two lower basins, nearly silted. Alongside, sharply contrasting, was a permanent funfair of roundabouts and shooting stalls, empty of patrons yet echoing with the traditional, never-varying sound of fair music. The scene was overlooked by the plain gaunt lines of the Tontine Hotel set on a simple lawn above the River Severn.

We walked along the river bank, shocked at the strength of the current which was carrying tree branches at a rapid pace, careering in the turbulent water. After months on the placid canals, the course of the river was frightening. We thought back to the warnings that we had been given about the problem of entering Gloucester docks. A mile below the town we reached Lincoln lock, designed for sea-going vessels and controlled by traffic lights, on an immense scale compared with the narrowbeam locks of the Staffs and Worcs. We thought about the fact that James Brindley never intended one of his canal boats to continue this way: in the past, there would have been a transhipment to a differently designed craft.

We had purposely selected June for the river part of our journey, but the next morning the sky was heavy with threatening clouds and the weather forecast was depressing. With the river already flowing high and fast, we were unwilling to enter it on a trip to Gloucester, perhaps taking three days, when there seemed to be a risk of flooding and the possibility that we would become bottled up at an unknown, perhaps remote point. We decided that it would be prudent to allow ourselves another day in Stourport to see which way the weather was going to turn.

We spent the day going to look at Bewdley. Walking through expansive riverside meadows, past a long line of private moorings for large motor cruisers (each with its own jetty and small garden), we reached the BWB sign indicating the official limit of navigation. A mile beyond, the river had cut dramatically past a sheer cliff of red sandstone, a ridge that continued inland, where there were signs of an earlier habitation, perhaps a hermit's cave.

About four miles from Stourport, we reached the graceful stone bridge and crossed over to Bewdley's waterfront, as fine as that of Henley-on-Thames yet sadly bereft of boats, deserted apart from a cluster of day-hire motor craft. It was a place designed for people to make use of the river and asking for boating activity. 'Save the Severn' placards from the previous weekend's demonstration against the navigation proposals were still flapping, unheeded, in the wind. Rain began to fall as we sought the lunchtime shelter of a pub.

That night *Frederick* was battered by a gale even within the comparative shelter of the basin and torrential rain fell at the river's source in the Welsh mountains. Although the next morning was bright and sunny in Stourport, a bleak factual notice posted in the lockkeeper's office confirmed our worst fears: LOCKS CLOSED – RIVER IN FLOOD. FIVE FEET ABOVE NORMAL

I called into the office to seek the lockkeeper's advice.

'Probably two or three days before the flooding slackens enough to open the river to navigation,' he replied. 'But, in a summer like this, no one can say for certain. You can have a fine day here in Stourport and think that the level is bound to drop, while it's teeming with rain in the Welsh mountains. It only takes a few hours to bring the water down, so conditions can change suddenly. I've never known a summer like this: it's the third or fourth time that the river's been closed in the past couple of months.'

We decided to cut our losses and put our programme in reverse. We had planned, originally, to reach Gloucester in June, returning up the Avon to Lapworth, where we would spend a week or two putting another top coat of paint over last summer's work before setting out towards the north-east. Now, in view of the Severn's uncertain conditions, we thought it advisable to return to Lapworth through Birmingham and from there, depending on the weather, decide whether to attempt the Severn again from the Avon and Tewkesbury, or to head directly northwards.

Although the change of plan meant covering part of the Staffs and Worcs again, we had the option of turning off it at Stourton and taking the Stourbridge canal almost into the centre of Birmingham: it looked an interesting variation.

I had not thought about maintenance stoppages in the summer, yet something prompted me to stop at a telephone box in Stourport while we were shopping for our departure. I rang the Canalphone information service that provided a recorded up-date on the official BWB list. Netherton tunnel – the vital link between the Stourbridge canal and the Birmingham mainline – was closed indefinitely, I discovered. It left us no choice but to return to Aldersley and ascend the Wolverhampton twenty-one-flight of which we had such unpleasant memories from the spring.

Passing through the bottom lock of the canal from Stourport's basin, we found that we were not the only ones affected by the weather; a disconsolate group of boaters had travelled inland from a hire base in Worcester, intending to complete a round holiday trip by returning down the Severn. The yard told them to stay in Stourport until they could be collected overland.

We thoroughly enjoyed our return cruise along the Staffs and Worcs, admittedly one of the most entrancing, intimate canals of the English network; it twisted and turned so much with such infinite variety that it had not been possible for us to appreciate it fully on the way to Stourport. We were grateful that circumstances had forced us to make the return journey, especially when we discovered that the abundant wild flowers had burst into a blaze of colour.

From Kidderminster, the canal had been cut along a line of red sandstone cliff, a sheer wall which at Austcliff overhung the route, creating an open-sided tunnel. As the cliff fell back from the waterway, steeply rising hillsides were covered in dense vegetation and trees of varied species: elegant lines of beeches interspersed with aristocratic oaks, a plantation of dark firs contrasting with a meadow bordered by regimented poplars and curtseying willows.

Under the trees, the rich soil gave root to a vibrant carpet of vivid bluebells and the deeper purple of great rhododendron bushes, many petalled heads as large as outspread hands falling indolently to the water's edge where the first sharp yellow spikes of iris were emerging. A scattering of bright pink stars could be made out among the high, waving heads of pristine white cow parsley.

The green vegetation embraced and engulfed the canal, reaching across from one side to the other, creating a natural leafy tunnel through which the sunlight glinted here and there. We felt like eighteenth-century landowners inspecting their expensively land-scaped park. It was beautiful and private. Yet, at Kinver, I climbed a steep hill from the village to the sturdy church to make a surprising discovery. Only a mile or so from the garden vale of the canal was the hard bleak outline of West Midlands housing estates, massed roofs and tower blocks.

Coming out of the green tunnel, we tied beneath Stourton Castle, where the St George's red and white flag fluttered from the tower – the birthplace in 1500 of Cardinal Poe who became Archbishop of Canterbury during the reign of Mary Tudor after Cranmer had been burned at the stake. A significant reminder that this part of England's green and pleasant land had known strife and friction in earlier days.

The next day, as the locks became more frequent, we became aware that the canal was pressing uphill. First, there was a pair of staircase locks at Botterham, followed at Bratch by one of the most picturesque set of three locks on the English waterways: in the middle was an octagonal toll-house with perfectly proportioned Georgian windows; beyond, a pumping-house with ornate painted turrets.

To the boater, Bratch presented a challenge not repeated any-where else on the English waterways. The three locks were placed close together with only a few feet of water separating them, yet they did not form a staircase in the recognised sense. Each one was a separate lock. Fortunately, there was a splendid lockkeeper in charge, standing on the bridge next to the toll-house, thoroughly enjoying his job of directing the progress of boats up and down these narrowbeam locks, giving orders in a stentorian voice that resounded from top to bottom.

After our slightly fraught previous experience of the Birmingham Canal Navigation – and, more to the point, its bad reputation among boaters for vandalism – we had decided to take our time in returning to Aldersley, arriving there at the bottom of the Wolverhampton flight on Monday morning. Meanwhile, on Sunday, we were reminded suddenly that the canals no longer belonged exclusively to boaters: from dawn, fishermen, released from months of frustrating immobility as the first day of the season opened, tramped heavily past *Frederick*, burdened with their bulky creaking gear. We rose to find a line of regularly spaced fishers on either side of the canal, the nearest ones seeming to be sitting almost on our bow and stern.

The alarm, once again, had been set for 6 a.m. for our return trip through Birmingham with the aim of reaching the comparative security of Gas Street by evening. In the grey light of dawn, Lynda found the paddles of the bottom lock of the Wolverhampton flight as heavy and difficult as she remembered, but before long we were not alone. Another boat, crewed by a party of eight adults, a sturdy Canadian couple and their English relatives, caught up rapidly with *Frederick*. Two of them went ahead to prepare locks in advance of the convoy. The Canadians were experienced in boating on the very different conditions of Lake Ottawa, yet they were thoroughly enjoying their first taste of the historic, heavily locked small English canal, so absorbed in the activity that they hardly seemed to notice the surrounding dereliction.

Arriving into the basin above the top lock, we were greeted by two enthusiastically bounding Alsatians, Lucy and Emma, followed by Ben and Cathy from *General Lee*: one of those unpredictable, surprise meetings that add to life on the waterways. Sadly, they were going in the opposite direction, about to descend the flight, yet there was enough time to exchange news of our experiences over the past months since last meeting at Long Buckby in the autumn.

We wanted to know how they had fared over the winter, as we had half expected to see them at Lapworth. After spending some time at Newbold outside Rugby on the north Oxford, they had moved towards Braunston just as the blizzard started. Although they had just reached the village, they became frozen into the ice away from any source of running water, and had had to carry supplies along the towing-path. The dogs became so used to crossing over the ice that when it started to break up Emma had accidentally fallen in. Ben dashed into the water to retrieve her. 'Cathy took her from me and rushed her into the warmth of the cabin,' Ben remarked ruefully. 'She just left me standing there, waist deep in freezing water!'

General Lee had passed through Birmingham on the previous day, Sunday, and Ben was upset by an incident when a gang of youths on a disused railway bridge had hurled bricks on to the boat. He found the going hard and tough, and warned about treacherous weeds and underwater objects – including, at one point, a submerged Mini car.

We departed in our different directions, and Lynda and I headed straight along the Birmingham mainline, this time passing across the junction with the Wyrley and Essington. At the top of the first set of three locks, I was hailed by a large, burly man.

'Are you going to Gas Street?' he asked. 'Can you give me a tow? Me boat's broken down.'

We hitched *Bella* on to *Frederick*'s stern. Since *Bella* was one of the smallest craft on the waterways – a cabin constructed over a short wooden hull, probably a former lifeboat – there was little drag. The only problem was that, being so lightweight, *Bella* swayed wildly and alarmingly from side to side in *Frederick*'s wash.

From time to time, Mr Bowyer disappeared from the stern into the high, narrow cabin to emerge shortly afterwards clutching a great hunk of sandwich and a mug of tea. On one occasion, *Bella* was left floundering without its skipper as we entered one of the narrow channels where, in the past, boats would have been weighed and paid tolls. *Bella* swung crazily, bouncing off the side, rolling dangerously, but Mr Bowyer appeared confidently unconcerned, waving an encouraging mug of tea.

Mr Bowyer worked for British Rail, a fact proudly proclaimed in his boat's decorations, which incorporated the BR symbol and Inter-City train stickers. As we progressed along the wide, straight canal, parallel with the mainline railway, passing trains gave hoots of recognition, accompanied by much shouting and arm-waving.

It was a relief to have such a convivial partner on our journey through Birmingham, and there were no signs of any trouble for us this time. Mr Bowyer enlivened the trip with comments shouted in a broad Brummagem accent above the roar of the engine: 'Over there, look right, you'll see the end of the Netherton tunnel.' 'This is Pudding Green junction.' 'We're now coming to Spon Lane junction where the old Wolverhampton level crosses over.' 'Here's Smethwick junction where the two levels join.' His enthusiasm for the BCN, strange and alien to me, was captivating and he made the system come alive as the unfamiliar names rolled off his tongue.

Taller city buildings enclosed the sides of the canal as we reached Farmers Bridge junction, where a signpost on an island gave the mileages to London, Worcester and Coventry. Mr Bowyer produced a brass hunting horn and heralded our arrival into Gas Street with trumpeting blasts that resounded and echoed through tunnels under buildings. People appeared from boats tied around this basin, one of the most traditional residential sites of the English canals, and greeted our friend. Rather sadly, we unhitched *Bella* and drifted away to a quiet mooring, surrounded by the dim shapes in the dusk of high-rise tower blocks, catching the background noises of a big city centre, the persistent murmur of a medley of traffic sounds.

It had taken six hours to traverse the thirteen-mile mainline system from Wolverhampton to Birmingham, and in Mr Bowyer's company it had been an enthralling experience.

It was late in the afternoon of the next day before we reached wellknown territory: the top lock of the north Stratford flight dropping into Lapworth.

During the morning, we had come through a different side of Birmingham, passing the extensive canalside frontage of the university campus, pinpointed by a slender brick campanile in the style of Florence and Siena. I felt that we should pause and explore the attractive park surrounding this seat of learning; it had been massively supported by public funds, so it seemed strange that signs forbade mooring 'without written notice'.

Bournville, Cadbury's nineteenth-century model factory in a garden village, also proved to be a disappointment: there was little sign of the waterfront where once a great fleet of narrowboats brought raw materials to manufacture the world-famous chocolate.

There was a great surprise and a great welcome for us on reaching the top lock of the Lapworth flight. Eric's head appeared over the side of the brick bridge, followed by encouraging waves and welcoming shouts. Although we had sent a card from Stourport reporting our change of plan and possible return, the timing of our arrival had been vague. His appearance at the exact moment that we returned was uncanny.

After the first two locks and a short pound, Eric reappeared at the top of 'the Thick', charging ahead, preparing locks as fast as we could descend, being joined towards the bottom of the flight by Ruth and Dan, wearing a smart red peaked cap and looking almost like a schoolboy.

We reached and tied on the Grand Union mainline at 6.30 p.m., some thirty-six hours after leaving Aldersley; we had travelled over thirty-four miles and passed through forty-four locks, our most intensive piece of boating to date. Although weary and exhausted by the effort, we were excited to return to the place that felt like home, where *Sandalwood* and *Frederick* had been tied, become iced in and survived the rigours of a severe winter.

Even so, it was no longer the place that we had known then: since we left it, the trees had come into leaf and the canalside foliage had thickened, the junction was thronged with hire boats, clamorous with the excitement of summer holidays. At that moment it seemed a strange, rather bewildering, life – that of a waterways gipsy. We had taken our own, much treasured, home and possessions on a journey to many different, unknown points in the north and west, and brought them back to a place that, earlier, seemed to belong to us. No longer did it feel that way.

There was another reason why Lapworth no longer felt like home. Eric and Ruth told us the sad story of how, soon after we had departed in March, they had been served three months' notice by the National Trust to quit their mooring in the top pound of the south Stratford canal. The remote, land-based bureaucrats may have had their own reasons for this, but it was a harsh decision to impose on someone who had lived in this place for sixteen years – one of the first boaters to take up the Trust's invitation of residential moorings – bringing up a family of three children and now responsible for the well-being of another small child. Moreover, Eric had really loved this place, made a delightful garden out of waste land,

and kept a constantly watchful, knowledgeable eye on the water conditions that he depended upon.

Despite valiant pleas, there seemed to be no hope of a change of heart from the National Trust. To avoid a situation of inevitably increasing bitterness, Eric and Ruth had opted for a new residential mooring in the Saltisford arm – once disused and now being reopened by a charitable trust with MSC backing – in Warwick.

Their move was lengthy, difficult and emotional. They had to dig up apple and plum trees which had become established on the canalside and replant them in the garden of the Warwick house owned by Eric's son. Then a sizable garden shed which provided a land base for many items of equipment had to be dismantled and re-erected in John's garden.

While this was going on, Lynda and I seized an opportunity of fine weather to reinforce our previous summer's work by giving another coat of paint to *Frederick*'s exterior.

Eric kept us in suspense about the day on which he would make the great move, torn between a reluctance to cut loose from Lapworth and the need to become established at the new base, but when Eric decides to move his boat, he moves it!

One morning, when the sun was clear overhead and the day looked so certain to be dry that I planned to work hard on *Frederick*, Eric started *Sandalwood*'s engine and told me that they were going to Saltisford. We waved until they were out of sight around the bend of the Grand Union, past the feathery larches; so sad that on the last occasion they had waved to *us* as we left in March for the north.

We completed the immediate painting, put the brushes in white spirit, clamped the tops on an array of paint tins, leaped into the car and drove furiously to the top of Hatton flight. We found that *Sandalwood* had already passed through the first three locks before the bend at the BWB workshops, and we joined them there, adjourning for much needed refreshment at the local pub.

From the mass of equipment on the boat, Eric produced a bicycle and I pedalled madly ahead, careering down the sharp inclines below each lock, opening them in advance. It was difficult to keep pace with the methodical, yet systematic way in which Eric handled his ninety-year-old boat, compared with *Frederick* too deep in draught for many contemporary conditions, yet relentlessly progressing down the flight of twenty-locks. We reached the bottom, with very little help from any ascending boats, in two and a half hours. *Sandalwood* was tied in the Saltisford arm, at that time unprepared for the arrival of its new residential craft.

Eric, Ruth, Dan and Sasha had moved, but there was one problem. Twpi, the peregrinating cat that we had looked after over a winter week, had disappeared at seeing his home removed. We drove back to Lapworth in Eric's car, found Twpi meandering desolately around, succeeded in catching him and bundled him, unceremoniously, into the car's boot. Sadly, we learned long afterwards that Twpi did not adjust to his new environment, had disappeared again and was never found. Perhaps there may be a small black cat, answering to the name of Twpi, wandering like Macavity around the Lapworth basin.

We returned to complete our work on *Frederick* and, once accomplished, spent our first week away from the boat in fourteen months, visiting Niki, my daughter, in the West Country, while Tony and Di Bird, living on *Latin Lady* at Knowle's bottom lock, kept a watchful eye on *Frederick*.

Then we set out on the second stage of our year's journey, returning towards the river Severn along the south Stratford canal, passing Eric's recently deserted mooring in the top pound. We spent two arduous days grappling with the demanding hard work of this canal, one that has been tainted with troublesome history.

Some twenty-five years ago, the south Stratford canal from Lapworth was effectively unnavigable. Over the previous quarter of a century it had become heavily silted, overgrown by weeds, its locks fallen into total disrepair; there had been no commercial traffic because the canal terminated at a dead end. The river Avon itself had become unusable from Evesham to Stratford a hundred years before.

Then, in 1958, Warwickshire County Council put forward a plan to lower a bridge at Wilmcote outside Stratford, which would have closed the canal to any future navigation. It became the focal issue which fired the imagination and enthusiasm of the embryonic canal restoration campaign, and started a ripple effect across the country which has gathered force ever since.

A Committee of Enquiry was set up to decide on the fate of the canal, and much of the debate centred on whether it would be cheaper to close it, as claimed by the British Transport Commission (at that time responsible for waterways), or to reopen it to navigation on a plan proposed by David Hutchings, a young architect working for Coventry Council, who became fascinated by the situation.

The support of the National Trust was enlisted to restore the canal, and the day was won with their backing. Nevertheless, victory hung on a single piece of paper: a receipt which proved that a canoe had passed through the canal during the previous year, evidence that the right of navigation existed and had been used.

The tremendous task, never before attempted elsewhere, was commenced of reopening the canal. BTC had stated that it would cost nearly £120,000 to close it; David Hutchings maintained that he could restore it for less than half of that sum. There were great pressures to keep within that budget, and it was achieved by engaging every available volunteer, making use of discarded lock equipment from other canals and enrolling the help of the Royal Engineers and of prisoners from Birmingham gaol.

David Hutchings – a man driven by a single ideal and intolerant of bureaucratic delays and interference – set a challenging timetable: the canal would be reopened within three years. His slogan was: 'Boats to Stratford-on-Avon before the Russians reach the Moon!' The date for the formal opening by Her Majesty the Queen Mother was fixed for 11 July 1964, and it had to be honoured.

Anyone appearing on the scene of frenetic activity was conscripted, as recorded by John Seymour in *Voyage into England* (David and Charles, 1966):

We came to a canal, silted up and with only a trickle of muddy water in it. We left the road and bumped along the towpath to where a gang of men were working with their shirts off, for it was a warm morning.

'Prisoners from Birmingham gaol,' said Hutchings.

They were working on a lock chamber, one side of which had been completely rebuilt of reinforced concrete. Deep down in the mud at the bottom was a huge pile of rubble from the old wall that had been blasted in.

'Got to get that shifted,' said David. 'Any good with a shovel?'

I felt like murmuring that I was better, actually, with a camera, but David is not the sort of man you murmur things like that to, or if you do he is apt to turn a deaf ear. . . .

One of the prisoners came and joined me. 'A free man's worth two pressed,' I quoted, to myself of course, but just how free was I? It is hard work shovelling a mixture of huge lumps of masonry, mixed with small lumps, mixed with tons of mud. The sun got higher in the sky and shone directly down into the narrow chamber, which was like an oven.

The prisoner and I sweated and swore. The prisoner got tired, and was relieved by another. I was not relieved. All I got was a pick-axe flung to me by David Hutchings during one of his mad dashes from here to there in the Land-rover. Prisoners came and prisoners went, but I went on for ever.

There are two curious appendices to this story of great achievement. The first concerns Stratford town council, which was well placed to enjoy the benefits of increased tourism from a whole new generation of leisure boating, yet gave little or no support to the scheme. Indeed, they had a plan, fortunately not carried out, to fill in Bancroft basin, the original commercial wharf, and transfer the canal junction with the Avon to another spot outside the town.

Secondly, the National Trust, originally a proponent of the canal's restoration, backed away from the situation, even though the navigation rights were transferred to it. Apart from taking on the river Wey in Surrey, the Trust's initial enthusiasm for waterways restoration faded fast, in sharp contrast to its campaign to preserve the British coastline. In recent years, navigation conditions on the Stratford have declined again, bringing about a situation of intense political pressure on the Trust to make up its mind about the future management of a canal which now forms a vital part of one of Britain's most popular waterways.

Emerging from the deep, low tunnel of the main road at Stratford into Bancroft basin, some fourteen months after our first visit, we felt that we were now almost fully fledged boaters, more knowledgeable about the English waterways, better informed about the struggles over the past thirty years to save them. I was looking forward to meeting David Hutchings in a few days' time on our way down the Avon.

The day was damp and chilly, typical of this summer, and the grass in front of the theatre was green, not parched and brown like a year ago; but the weather did not affect the tourists, still milling in massed crowds, gongoozling at a boat passing through the lock. Even before we had tied, a lady was asking for help in locating her hotel boat. Others stopped to ask: 'Can you take me for a trip along the canal?' 'Where's the river go to?' 'Is that a genuine old longboat?'

The basin was packed with boats and we squeezed into the side arm, close to a cruiser called *Kippin Two*. Bearded Brian Morgan glanced at the threatening clouds and remarked, 'I don't like the look of the weather at all.'

He explained that he acted, in his spare time, as Master of the Reach at Fladbury lock on the Lower Avon, which was administered from Evesham to Tewkesbury by a trust depending to a large extent on the voluntary efforts of its members. Each lock was supervised by people like Brian who spent their weekends checking on local conditions and carrying out minor maintenance work.

The river had become unnavigable from Pershore during the Second World War and the rights were purchased from a moribund company by Douglas Barwell, who set up the Lower Avon Navigation Trust some thirty-five years ago. Restoration by voluntary working groups was steady, though slow, and the river was reopened to a point east of Evesham in 1964, coinciding with the more rapid renewal of the Stratford canal, the two events marking a significant turning point in the recent history of the English waterways.

David Hutchings had turned his energies to recreating a through route, though it seemed an almost impossible task when the Upper Avon Navigation Trust was formed in 1965. This part of the river had been unnavigable since 1872; only two weirs remained, no locks had survived, and rights of access to the river were limited. Fund-raising was the initial urgent task, much helped by a substantial anonymous donor; work began in 1969 and the link was completed within five years, a truly amazing effort.

On our first night back in Bancroft basin it rained heavily, continuing into the next day. Brian Morgan went to check the level of the river and reported ominously that it was rising. 'As soon as there's a break, I'm going to make back down river to Fladbury while it's still open; I can't afford to be cut off by possible flooding.'

This was starting to look like a repetition of our experience six weeks ago in Stourport, and we began to wonder about the state of the Severn. However, the next day the rain ceased and a watery sun filtered through the clouds as we dropped from the canal on to the Avon.

Carried by a strongish stream, we slipped down the river at a fast pace, soon passing Welford and steering cautiously through the single navigable arch of the ancient stone bridge at Bidford, where manicured lawns from splendid houses edged the river. We passed through a succession of large widebeam locks with good modern mechanism, set in attractive landscaped surroundings, planned for boaters' needs of water and rubbish disposal, affirming UANT's outstanding record of steady improvement year after year, which has turned the Upper Avon into Britain's model waterway. We noticed new extensions since the previous year to moorings in the lock entrances – so important on this river where the waterside seemed to propagate 'No Mooring' signs – equipped with tall steel posts and roving rings to give protection against flooding. The Trust was clearly run by people who understood boating and, at the same time, wished to live in harmony with their neighbours.

We tied at the lock named Robert Aickman, commemorating one of the original founders of the Inland Waterways Association, where a new channel had been cut past an old mill on an island, by-passing a previously awkward right-angled turn below the weir – another of the improvements over the last few years.

The next day, a Land-rover came bounding across a rough track to the lock. David Hutchings leaped out, jumped on board *Frederick* and talked breathlessly for two hours about his plans for reopening the Severn, as well as the possibility of extending the Avon navigation from Stratford to Warwick, thus forming for the first time a direct widebeam link with the Grand Union. Bright-eyed, dynamic, enthusiastic, inexhaustible, he spoke of his battles with the authorities and conservationists, a man who has had a mission over twenty-five years, still uncompleted, to raise the standard of English waterways and bring more of our heritage within access of ordinary people. He disappeared as he had arrived, at the same speed and in a cloud of dust.

Afterwards, we needed time to absorb all that he had told us, and reflect over his plans in a quiet walk. We were on the same mooring next morning when the Land-rover careered back to the lock, David

Hutchings leaped out and started to clear the rubbish from the bins since the person assigned to this job was late in arriving. My respect for this man of vision was increased when I realised that he had such a work-a-day, practical attitude of mind.

At Evesham, the frontier post between the two navigation trusts, an ultra-modern triangular house was occupied by the lockkeeper. He helped *Frederick* to pass through the shortest lock on the river by angling the boat across the full width and nudging out through both gates. We were just able to make it.

'If you're going to Gloucester, do you know about the entrance to Llanthony lock?' he enquired helpfully. 'It's very tricky and you need to be prepared. You come down this narrow sidestream, and just beyond the lock is an unprotected weir. If the lock isn't open, you've got to get a line on to the high wall on the left before the lock. Now, if it's any use to you, what I've done is to attach a steel grappling hook to a chain on the stern of my boat; hook that on to one of the ladders on the wall and you'll be safe while you look around.'

We thanked him for his advice, though wondering if we wanted any more warnings to add to those from Andy Millward back in Ellesmere Port and several other boaters on the way down. Did we, any longer, wish to reach Gloucester at all?

Meanwhile, it seemed unlikely that there would be any chance of entering the Severn at all, as the weather deteriorated once again; there was a day of raging gales at Pershore and we watched the river rise from our precarious mooring on a water-logged meadow.

Two days later, passing through a narrow arch of King John's bridge at Tewkesbury, the smallest opening on the Avon, we reached the lock above the Severn. Believing that we would be winding round and returning upstream, I went to a telephone box and called the keeper at Upper Lode, the lock a mile below Tewkesbury on the Severn.

'There's a bit of stream running on the river and it's rising,' he reported. 'But you should be all right tomorrow, there's little tide, so the conditions should be quite good. I'll look out for you tomorrow.'

At the marina I purchased two steel hooks, attaching them to chains at the bow and stern. I felt that we were prepared as well as we could be for our arrival, at long last, on the river Severn.

Chapter Nine

Sharpness to Stourport

'Have you thought that we're going on to a fairly remote part of the waterways?' I remarked to Lynda, the evening before we left Tewkesbury. 'Like the Nene last year, I should imagine that we will see few other boats.'

It was one of several misconceptions about the Severn, and the Gloucester and Sharpness canal, which I had formed in advance and which were to be proved incorrect. As *Frederick* swung out of the quiet backwater channel below Tewkesbury lock and into the wide expanse of the Severn, lashed into waves by a fierce wind, I found that I had been wrong about my first prediction. A large sea-going cruiser, radio and radar masts sprouting from its upper deck, surged ahead towards Upper Lode lock. Hugging the far side to avoid the unprotected weir stretching across the river, we arrived in front of the lock to find several more boats holding to the posts.

The great gates started to swing open and we entered the immense lock designed for substantial freighters in the days when there had been commercial trade to Worcester. Like flies on a wall, we clung to chains hanging from the sides, next to a small twenty-five-foot river cruiser.

As we began to drop, foot by foot, a woman on the deck told me that they had experienced waves breaking over their bow coming downstream from Upton-on-Severn.

'Have you been this way before? Have you entered Gloucester docks?' I asked her.

'Yes, about three times, and I'm always glad when it's over.'

'I've heard about the problems of the approach wall,' I replied. 'Can you have give us any useful advice?'

'It's not all that bad, just a matter of getting a line on to it – otherwise you're carried over the weir beyond.' Then, looking at *Frederick*'s length, she added, 'Mind you, you should be all right as the channel is so narrow – at worst you would end up straddled across the stream!'

I was not certain whether to be reassured by her advice or not. There was no time to contemplate it, however. The towering gates at the far end opened, and ahead lay the vast river stretching into the distance; the large cruisers surged out, followed by *Frederick* and the small cruiser.

We came out into an expanse of water like a small sea with rollers breaking in regular lines from side to side, *Frederick*'s bow lifting over them, then planing down. I was comforted by the easy way in which the long boat designed for narrow canals settled to the rolling pattern, and it was exhilarating to watch the bow wave curling past the hull. The sea-going cruisers steamed away out of sight along the straight section of river, the smaller one gradually opening a gap between us but staying almost in view for most of the trip. Many craft were coming upstream, their bows cutting dramatically through the choppy water.

Even out in mid-stream, the banks were too high for us to see the immediate surroundings, but there was a fine background of scenery, slowly changing as we progressed. At first, the sturdy square tower of Tewkesbury's Norman abbey was revealed across open meadows; behind rose the solitary mass of Bredon Hill which had dominated so much of the landscape on the lower part of the Avon. A sharp escarpment of the Cotswolds took over on the left; finally, straight ahead, Wainhope hill grew in stature, its steeply rising slope green with grass which looked as smooth as a lawn, capped by a dense clump of trees.

About three hours after leaving Upper Lode and some three miles outside Gloucester, the main river turned away sharply to the right; ahead, the navigation channel narrowed to roughly the size of a widebeam canal, winding through the outskirts of the city. Keeping a close check on the map, we passed under a railway bridge and two road bridges, and turning a corner I saw the high curved stone wall of the approach to the lock.

Acting on the warning advice that I had been given, I reduced the engine to its lowest effective speed, edged along the wall until the hull was hugging it, held the grappling iron ready in one hand and successfully hooked it on to a rung of the first ladder. We secured in the fast-flowing stream. Then I looked ahead to the lock, 100 yards away, and saw that the gates were standing prepared and open with a green light showing. This day, we had been fortunate in our timing and need not have taken all the precautions. On entering, we joined the same band of fast cruisers that had charged ahead of us from Upper Lode; due to their earlier arrival, the lock had been standing ready for *Frederick*.

A splattering of tourists in colourful summer clothes peered from the top into the deep lock as the boats started to rise high above the river to the level of the Gloucester and Sharpness canal, and the fascinating scene of Llanthony dock opened before us like a curtain rising on a stage setting: tall narrow brick warehouses with high pitched roofs, evocative of the Hanseatic towns, ringed the handsome basin and the picture was framed by the towering masts, crossbeams and rigging of a wooden barque, romantically recreating the departed splendours of the port.

While the cruisers slipped out of the lock to join lines of other modern white craft around the quays, the keeper said to me, 'You'd be best over on the far side of the basin; pass under the road bridge.' As we pottered slowly across the large basin, I began to wonder if I had understood his instructions. City road traffic was pouring over a bridge standing only about three feet above water level. 'Pass under the bridge – are you sure that's what he said?' I ruminated. 'What do we do now?'

Warning bells clanged harshly, barriers descended at either end halting the flow of vehicles, and the bridge started to pivot upwards, cantilevered in Dutch style. As Gloucester's traffic ground to a halt, we felt very privileged to be passing under the bridge.

On the far side we tied to a wharf under the colonnaded arcade of a disused warehouse, a short distance in front of another narrow-boat, *Wyton*. George leaped out of it and came to help us.

'My advice is move back as far as you can from the edge of the building,' he shouted. 'There's broken guttering above, and water jets out when it rains. It happened to me, our first night here, and I had to get up at 3 a.m. to move the boat as we couldn't stand the thundering noise on the roof!'

From scudding rain in the early morning, the day had broadened into clear sunny skies and – for the first time in many days – we sat outside, sipping wine and admiring the glorious sunset over Llan-thony dock, glimpsing the white ornate wedding-cake tracery of the cathedral tower, hearing from George and Ruby of their five years living afloat. Both of them had retired from the RAF with Ruby's one condition that she would not cook another meal; every day, they went out to lunch and in the evening George served a cold meal.

Seagulls of enormous wing-span circled and dived overhead, screeching and crying like alley cats. Their weird, harsh noise was overtaken during the night by the steady pattering of rain, shortly followed by a thunderous jet plunging over *Frederick*'s bow, but not quite hitting the cabin roof. George had been right!

Work began in 1794 on the canal from Gloucester, originally intended to terminate at the small port of Berkeley. Increasing traffic from the Midlands canals, including the Staffs and Worcs, had created demand to provide a safer and more economical route which would by-pass the treacherous part of the Severn where the famous Bore reaches its height.

After cutting five miles from Gloucester, the scheme ran out of funds and remained dormant and useless until Telford was commissioned in 1817 to make a fresh study of the project. As usual, he decided to cut a corner, designating a new terminal on the spit of land at Sharpness, and ten years later the Gloucester and Sharpness canal was opened after massive government funding to create work for the nineteenth-century unemployed. The canal was at that time the broadest and deepest in the world.

My second misconception was that this canal, being the first one designed for shipping that I had travelled on, would be dead straight and boring. Indeed, we set out in the belief that we would spend only a few days on it, mainly for the sake of saying that we had reached Sharpness. Once again, I found that I was wrong.

Setting out from Gloucester on the day of the annual rowing regatta, taking place on the first section of canal outside the city, we had to thread our way cautiously through a chaos of more boats than, we felt, could have taken part in Henley's event. It seemed as though the organisers did not realise that the canal was used by seventy-foot narrowboats. There were few signs of any controlling authority as we edged along one side on which pairs and sculls were negotiating towards their starting position, while on the other side eights were racing desperately to their winning point, many crewed by delectable young ladies.

Now we had to work our way through the succession of twelve lift-and-swing bridges over the sixteen miles of the canal. The Sharpness had no locks, yet each bridge was controlled by a keeper who regulated traffic with red and green warning lights. Although some of the bridges would have been high enough to allow *Frederick* to pass beneath without difficulty, the rules of this shipping canal were strictly enforced to ensure that there was no possibility of a collison, and the bridge-keepers were only on duty during certain, published, working hours.

This canal, unlike any other we had yet encountered in England, was still maintained to the standard required for commercial transport. Rightly so, I discovered, as another misconception was turned on its head.

On a misty morning, we heard the heavy, dull throb of powerful engines approaching along the canal. I raised the front canopy, dripping with water, and peered into the dim distance where, vaguely, I could make out a vast shape approaching. As a German cargo vessel reached us, towering overhead, figures seen dimly on the top deck, *Frederick* was surging and bouncing in the immense swell of its progress. It passed along, throbbing engines dying away on the mist, its wash carrying *Frederick* excitedly backwards and forwards.

Yet another misconception bit the dust as I discovered that the countryside around the Sharpness was unusually beautiful. As the long ridge of the Cotswolds fell away behind Gloucester, the immediate surroundings were flat with lush meadows, full of rich dairy herds, golden cornfields and small dark woods on either side, yet the hills were never far away. After Saul junction, where the small, low swing-bridge was operated by a keeper leaning on it like a lock beam, the canal came closer to the Severn estuary, a silver sheen of water glistening in the distance a mile or two towards the Monmouthshire hills, surrounded by dark green trees. On a flat plain on the other side of the canal stood the lovely Gloucestershire village of Frampton: a long straggling line of old stone and deep redbrick houses, a fine Georgian manor house in a park, the church set apart at one end among willows in a water meadow – the quintessence of English scenery.

Between Sharpness and Purton the last two miles of canal were carried on an embankment immediately alongside and above the river, nudging the walls at high tide, giving way at low tide to a desert of sand and mud flats, a few solitary fishermen digging here and there for bait and collecting their catch from nets and baskets – a trade going back into the recesses of history, often fraught with danger and foul weather. The hills on the far side dropped more steeply to the banks and, nestling in a crevice, the ancient port of Lydney – once a major shipbuilding centre where the great wooden men-of-war were constructed to fight against the Spanish Armada.

The sloping sides of the embankment at Purton had become a forlorn graveyard for row after row of former Severn sailing trows which had been driven into the ground, their skeleton hulks rising at odd angles like leaning gravestones.

We tied below Purton opposite one of several ponds edged with tall feathery reeds, originally used for storing timber; a thin line of thorn bushes gave some shelter from a wind that was rising to gale force along the estuary and sending waves rolling down the canal.

By the following morning, *Frederick* was being rocked and bashed by breakers as though on the sea, and we were glad to be tied firmly to bollards, provided throughout the length of the Sharpness. It was the weekend of the Fastnet race in which many vessels perished at sea. We were expecting Sunday visitors from Swansea and I battled against the wind to the village telephone box.

'Roger, I wonder if you realise what a gale is blowing here. Do you think it wise to come over, as the Severn bridge will probably be closed?'

Roger was not the kind of person to be put off easily from what he had planned to do, so he and Elizabeth arrived at Purton, though an hour later than intended because of long queues caused by restrictions on the bridge.

After they left, the evening, as so often happens in the west, turned into a glorious clear sunset and we continued to Sharpness marina on a peninsula projecting into the estuary, yet protected by a miniature Rock of Gibraltar – a perfect picture of many fine craft floating in the calm reflection of a pale blue sky tinged with orange. On the far side of the hill, facing towards the sea, the commercial docks were lined by high, gaunt cranes, frozen into immobility like watchful herons waiting patiently, absolutely still, for a catch.

Walking through the docks the next day, we saw several cranes bending and bobbing under the weight of cargo lifted from the three or four ships in port. We continued beyond the line of exposed houses built above the edge of the estuary and along an embankment towards the massive square bulk of Berkeley nuclear power station – the world's first – and the distant outline of the Severn bridge.

We took an inland path across fields up to the historic town of Berkeley, once designated as the canal's terminus, though now the river, which 200 years ago provided a port, had become silted. The town had grown up around a square with a small cluster of shops, and on its edge we found the lofty and imposing church containing almost perfect marble effigies of medieval knights and their ladies, alongside the stark fortified castle where Edward II was murdered in 1327. The feudal stronghold has remained in the Berkeley family since the twelfth century, which must be something of a record.

The course of history has been changed more than once by events in this modest town. In the early nineteenth century, Dr Edward Jenner, who lived in an immaculate, stately Georgian house close to the church, pioneered many medical treatments, among them the discovery – which altered the life cycle of mankind – of inoculation as the prevention of smallpox.

In the Mariner's Arms the portly publican was presiding over convivial lunchtime company, including the skipper of a Westerley twenty-six-foot yacht, then moored at Ilfracombe, who was exchanging sea-faring stories with an ex-Royal Naval officer. At Berkeley, there was the scent of salt air, tides and storms – a long way from the pollution of some Midlands canals, yet directly linked with them.

Overhead, lifelike puppet witches dangled from the bar, a reminder of a long-held belief in witchcraft that has survived in Berkeley.

Returning back along the canal towards Gloucester, we stopped at Patch bridge, once a settlement of shepherds who watched silently over their flocks on the marshes, now the place to which waterfowl experts flock in their thousands every year to watch intently from secluded hides the migration habits of swans and geese. From a remote house where Peter Scott first started to observe and paint his famous pictures of water birds in flight, now adorning the walls of millions of homes, Slimbridge has developed into the world's centre for the study of waterfowl and the largest international collection of these birds.

On a September day, when the road was jostling with cars and coaches, we walked to Slimbridge with some misgivings, fearful that it would be like any other zoo, populated by sad, frightened captives, shy of visitors.

After staying an hour beyond the official closing time we left enthralled by what we had seen, another misconception blown away. Admittedly, the pool around the reception and exhibition centre was a bit like Regent's Park with its massed quacking ducks and hoards of sightseers, but we left this part quickly and discovered peaceful natural grounds so extensive that we could cover only half of them, quite rapidly, in an afternoon. Except for a few rare tropical species kept in a hothouse, there were no pens or cages and, although each type of bird had a reserved area, they were so free to roam that they often strayed elsewhere.

The variety of ducks, geese and swans came as a stunning revelation – we had had no idea that there were so many variations in colouring, shape and size, type of beak and plumage. We became absorbed and entranced in trying to identify each new individual that we met scurrying along the paths or flapping in the water. We saw the cosmetic Carolina duck, the red-nosed rosybill, the shovellers with their spade-like beaks, the subtle brown markings of teals, the amazing diving of black and white scaups. We learned that a 'goose' can sometimes be a duck and that geese can range from pygmies to giants, some with pink feet, others with red breasts; we found that some swans never turn snowy white and remain proudly black with a scarlet beak; we heard that not all water birds quack, there are some that chuckle and others that whistle.

The half-day originally allocated to Slimbridge proved to be totally inadequate; we had to return for a second visit, and both of us became Trust members (giving free and unlimited access not only to Slimbridge itself, but also to six other reserves now set up in other parts of Britain). We climbed to the top of wooden towers, swinging in the wind, to look over the desolate marshes, and strolled through wetlands created to provide a natural environment and food for the waterfowl, and on to secretive hides from which, at the right time of the year, enthusiasts observe the migration of Slimbridge's pride and joy, Bewick swans and Brent geese, many ringed and sponsored by individuals so that their lifestyle can be studied more precisely.

Although we searched long and hard, we could not find the most spectacular of ducks, the mandarin, designed like a technicolour Chinese junk, so we were delighted when, two months after visiting Slimbridge, we identified a pair on the river Thames. Since our visit to the Wildfowl Trust our eyes have been opened to, and our senses become more acutely aware of, the range of water birds in Britain, adding enormously to the pleasure of boating.

Our first sighting occurred on the way back along the canal to Gloucester: an extraordinary hook-nosed creature, almost like a pterodactyl from the Lost World, emerged from the water, its heavy wide wings flapping on the water in an effort to make height, then hovering overhead like a witch and swooping down into the water on its prey. It must have been a cormorant and it continued to trail and haunt us on our way into Gloucester.

At Saul junction we paused to delve into canal history. This had been a waterways crossroads where the Thames and Severn canal – once providing a marvellous link from Lechlade on the Thames right through to the Severn – passed across the Sharpness. A year or so earlier, we had seen the extant original arm of the canal at Lechlade. Now we walked along a short section at Saul still used for permanent moorings.

Beyond the junction there remained a pair of decaying wooden lock-gates, after which the line of the canal had been filled in, although we could trace its course clearly along the ridge of the former towing-path until we reached a final section, close to the Severn, where tall reeds and yellow waterlilies were growing in the cut. Further east, between Stroud and Cirencester in the Cotswolds, the canal had passed through Sapperton tunnel, the longest at 3,808 yards ever bored in Britain and one of the many obstacles to the canal's restoration, although there is a hard core of enthusiasts who believe that this will be achieved some time in the next century.

From the extraordinarily long village of Frampton, we walked across fields to another disused canal, the Cambridge, a surprise since I did not know that there was any other Cambridge outside East Anglia or Boston, USA. A weatherbeaten farmer, sitting comfortably inside the protected cabin of his tractor, was rounding up a herd of Friesians and he stopped to answer some of the questions that had perplexed us in travelling around the countryside.

'Cows with collars? They need extra vitamin cake and the collar activates a computer that controls the level of food supply.'

'A rainy summer like this? It's what we're used to in these parts and it's good for me, it makes the grass grow so that I can get a second hay crop and I don't have to give extra feed – not like summa the farmers around here who thought they could get on the EEC bandwagon and grow grain – a curse on 'em.'

'Bulls? Yes, I keep a bull, but only so's 'e can get at those cows that 'aven't come pregnant through AI. They're like us, sum become pregnant all the time, sum not at all,' he added with a wry grin. 'Artificial insemination is cheaper at six quid a go, but it's always difficult to hit the right time, so a bull's useful for going and mopping up.'

'A bull? He can handle about twenty heifers over six weeks – and good luck to 'im, s'what I say.'

Instead of the planned two or three days on the 'boring' Sharpness canal, we spent some three weeks, enjoying the variety of sights, the deep clear water and fine moorings. Where else, I asked, can you find sixteen miles of lock-free wide and deep water with easy mooring close to pubs and historic places, set in a lovely environment where the people speak in the warm broad tones of the West Country? Even so, in September, we had many days when driving rain forced us to stay where we were tied, and there was barely a single hot sunny day.

The wind was still blowing fiercely when we returned to the same mooring next to the arcaded warehouse at Gloucester, and in turning I underestimated its force, blowing straight down the canal. *Frederick* was caught side on and, as we tried to avoid the danger of being blown towards the lift bridge, the bow fender hit one of *Wyton*'s windows. As it was made from toughened glass like a car's windscreen, the slight impact immediately shattered the window. I was stunned that, for the first time, I had damaged another boat.

Alan rushed from *Minstrel V*, also moored nearby, to help and Barbara made coffee to console me. George and Ruby were out at lunch, so I had to spend an hour or so waiting in dreadful suspense for their return, preparing my apologies.

They were generously understanding and sympathetic. 'Don't worry about it – it must have been worse for you than me,' George said, very graciously.

The damage, fortunately, was repaired within twenty-four hours since there was a specialist glazier's shop in the next street. Even so, it had been an object lesson to me about the inherent, potential dangers in boating, so easily overlooked in the pleasures, and – like a motorist after a first driving accident – I have become even more careful in handling the boat, particularly when conditions are difficult.

Alan and Barbara gave great support over the accident. 'It could have happened to anyone in those conditions,' was their philosophy. They were working from dawn to dusk, and sometimes later, in completely refitting a newly acquired twin-screw cruiser which they planned to take across the Channel in the autumn and down the French canals to the Mediterranean. They had no fears about the trip as they had both spent several years driving giant container vehicles from Merseyside through Europe to the Middle East, and they had had many experiences of breakdowns and other incidents, including one night spent in a Turkish gaol. Sadly, Alan had sustained an accident in which his head had been severely injured; although now full recovered, he had given up work and they had bought a small boat on which they had travelled the Midlands canals before embarking on the more ambitious project.

Their task on *Minstrel V* was completed soon afterwards, and the day before we left Gloucester they departed on a test run, the cruiser's powerful engines driving it on to the crest of a wave.

We followed at a more leisurely pace, dropping back on to the Severn from Llanthony lock – no problems going upstream – on a day when the sun at last, for the first time in many weeks, was hot enough to encourage me to strip down to shorts, even though there was still a keen cross wind.

The unaccustomed, relaxing warmth must have contributed to my loss of attention as we progressed up the middle of the great river; also, switching on the bilge pump as a routine exercise, I was alarmed when a jet of dark black fluid appeared, colouring the water like diesel. Was there a leak in the fuel supply? Peering into the engine room, I suddenly realised that I had not checked on our direction and, looking up, found that we were heading straight for the side. Too late! We ground into mud immediately below the remaining entrance gates of the former Coombe Hill canal.

It was one of the times when we have felt that *Frederick* has a mind of his own. Perhaps he felt an evocative pull to return to a long-past canal age. At any rate, on this day we landed in thick sludge, the wind battering the boat on to the shore, and we had the nearly impossible task of shafting off the boat from the side and back on course.

A few miles upstream at Lower Lode pub, we spotted some good new pontoon moorings – a rarity on the Severn – and tied there. Once again, I delved into the engine room to check on the bilge problem. There was nothing apparently wrong with the fuel pipes and connection so I concluded that there was no serious fault, simply some spillage from the separate tray under the engine. Meanwhile, I could hear Lynda talking animatedly with the people from the next boat.

Ken and Lucy, and their two glamorous young daughters with flowing blonde hair, came from Gloucester. After our thoroughly enjoyable and interesting stay in the area, we were delighted to make personal contact with people who lived locally and knew the river well.

'It's as unpredictable as a beautiful woman, calm and loving one day, raging and angry the next,' said Ken. 'You need to know what you're doing. Every year there are fatal accidents at Gloucester docks, and where I go fishing for eels and elvers on the mud flats further down, people often get lost.'

I had been trying to find out how far the river up to Tewkesbury was tidal.

'There can be a rise and fall as much as fourteen feet at times,' replied Ken, 'and when a spring tide is running boats can go straight over the weir at Upper Lode.'

We were sitting inside Ken's converted ex-Royal Naval lifeboat, the wooden hull of curved white planking floated lightly on the water, bobbing and rocking in the swell of the water.

Looking out of a porthole, we saw *Minstrel V* speeding past, Alan sitting happily at the wheel as it sliced through the water leaving a deep wake behind.

'Do you know how long it takes a boat to sink?' asked Ken. 'I had a previous boat that sprung a tiny leak when we were out in midstream. Even baling hard with two pails and setting straight for shore, the water poured in and the boat was full and sinking by the time we grounded. It's frightening how quickly it can happen.'

That evening, under a canopy of twinkling stars and a full silver moon, I was sitting outside, enjoying the clear tranquil night, when I became aware that there was something thrashing noisily under the hull, banging against the side and pushing hard enough to move the boat. Then a gleaming black shape glided away, snaking through the water and leaping above it, splashing in the luminescence. Other people watching it from the bank believed that it was a small seal that had come up-river and established itself around that place.

The next morning we set out up-river, passing under the 170-foot single-span Mythe bridge, constructed from cast iron to Telford's design in 1828, and catching the first magic view of the sharp, blue ridge of the Malverns. The river was almost straight until, about two hours after leaving Tewkesbury, we turned a bend and saw Upton-on-Severn ahead, its fine waterfront and cupola clocktower giving an impression, at this distance, of an Italian lakeside town.

As I slowed to scan for a mooring long enough to accommodate *Frederick*, there was a strident shout from the opposite bank. Alan appeared through some bushes, frantically waving his arms.

'*Minstrel*, the blasted boat, nearly sank!' he screamed. He crawled along a pole connecting a toilet disposal pontoon and managed to clamber on board.

'What do you mean, it nearly sank?' I queried. 'We saw you steaming by at Upper Lode – everything looked fine.'

'That's it, we'd had a splendid trip to Sharpness and then up here; the boat was performing beautifully. Then, just as we came to tie here, water began to gush through one of the propeller shafts. It was pouring in so fast that we just managed to get into the marina and beach it on the slipway before it would have sunk.'

On hoisting the boat out of the water and on to joists in the yard, they found that a rubber seal around the shaft had been faulty. Alan had spent several hours telephoning all over the country for a replacement, eventually locating one in Chichester.

'I've had enough of this troublesome boat,' said Alan. 'After all the work I've put into it, this happens. I'm fed up. I'm going to sell it as soon as possible and buy a narrowboat.'

We learned much later that he did exactly that, and Barbara and he have lived on *Harvey* and travelled widely through the inland waterways.

We spent the next day with Barbara, wandering around the narrow, congested streets of Upton, while Alan drove to Chichester and back. Then we progressed up-river for another two hours to Worcester, tying below the great east rose window of the sandstone cathedral. The river was busy with sleek rowing eights in brightly painted boats powered by skilled crews; from the opposite banks, sounds carried of the hard smack of a cricket ball on willow followed by the huge shouts of a large crowd, as Worcestershire competed in a crucial one-day match.

Stepping off *Frederick*, we walked under a medieval archway and climbed above the river to a garden glowing with summer flowers under the cathedral walls. In the opposite direction, we strolled to Diglis basin, packed with great sea-going cruisers cheek-by-jowl with narrowboats, reflecting its position as the junction with the Worcester and Birmingham canal, ascending to the Midlands through Tardebigge, England's longest flight of locks. By the bottom lock, we saw the attractive Elizabethan building, the Commandery, which served as the headquarters of the young Charles II in the final defeat of the Royalist cause by Cromwell in 1651.

We set out, once more, up-river against a fairly strong stream, the river becoming more enclosed with thick bushes and trees on either side.

Approaching the Burf, where I had thought of mooring for the night, there was a forty-five-foot narrowboat caught under the trees and the couple on board were waving wildly.

'We've broken down – please can you give us a tow?' they shouted.

Against the fast-running stream, it was difficult to manoeuvre alongside under the mass of overhead branches. Eventually, we managed to tie the boats together, bow and stern, and started out towards Stourport, making slow headway against the current.

Terry told us that he had borrowed *Tameris* for a week from his brother; from the outset, the engine had tended to dwindle and fail after it had been running for an hour or so. 'A good thing you came along when you did,' he remarked gratefully. 'There've been few boats about and we had signalled already to a cruiser, but they said they would not have sufficient power to tow us.'

At Lincomb, the top lock on the river, we explained the situation to the keeper and asked if he could telephone ahead to Stourport so that, breasted up, we could pass through the widebeam locks into the safety of the basin.

When we arrived, twenty minutes later, the gates were as usual padlocked. I steered the pair of boats as close to the alternative narrowbeam locks as possible, cast off *Tameris*, its engine now just ticking over, and watched anxiously to ensure that they made the entrance, while trying to hold *Frederick* steady on the stream. The lock entrance was awkward and tricky under the best conditions, and there was always the problem that there could be another boat already descending the staircase.

After circling around for long enough to give *Tameris* time to ascend, we entered the flight and Joan returned to help us through, reporting that they had reached a safe point in the lower basin.

We returned to the upper basin below the bottom lock of the Staffs and Worcs canal, to the mooring where two months earlier we had sat and waited for the river flood to abate. At last we had achieved our aim of travelling along the full length of the navigable Severn from Sharpness to Stourport, though the last few days seemed to have been a chapter of accidents.

Epilogue

The long way back

We left Stourport on a Saturday when the streets were closed to normal traffic, taken over for the fortieth annual Land and Water Festival by an endless snaking convoy of lorries ingeniously converted to colourful, entertaining tableaux, while boats in the basin were bedecked with bunting and lights for the evening's parade on the Severn.

We had two months left to make our way back to Rickmansworth and *Frederick*'s winter mooring, when we would return to reoccupy the Islington house. The six months' extension of the tenancy expired in early November and this time it would not be renewed, partly because we wished to repossess the house and prepare it for selling in the coming spring.

For the second time, we returned along the Staffs and Worcs, the garden vale now transformed by the darker shades of late summer, the banks deep in the pinky-mauve, delicate petals of Himalayan balsam. At Aldersley, we continued towards the canal's aristocratic climax – Tixall Wide – where it opened to lake-like proportion, the edges deep in high, feathery pale reeds, overlooked by the turreted Elizabethan gatehouse, a life-sized version of a child's toy castle.

Early on a September morning, as an enlarged ball of red sun burned through light mist rising over the lake, we continued to the junction with the Trent and Mersey at Great Haywood, where part of the village street extended to an ancient narrow packhorse bridge, crossing the swift sparkling river Sow, and connected with the entrance to Shugborough Hall, once the home of the earls of Lichfield.

The canal passed under a more recent ornate iron bridge which the Anson family built so that they could arrive at church by carriage, rather than walk 300 yards over the public crossing. Just beyond, there was a fine view of the handsome façade of the seventeenth-century neo-Classical mansion set in a beautiful land-scaped park at the foot of Cannock Chase.

Now we were progressing eastwards along a section of the Trent and Mersey that we had not travelled over during the past sixteen months. There was no definite plan for the remaining two months; although York, sadly, was beyond our reach this year, I was still hoping to gain some experience of the river Trent by going as far as Newark, even perhaps to Lincoln, before returning along the river Soar and the Grand Union to Rickmansworth.

The canal followed the course of the river Trent, quite small and polluted in its upper reaches, the landscape dominated by the vast integrated coalmine and power station at Rugeley, where the Chamber of Commerce had thoughtfully erected a sign to welcome boaters – unfortunate that it was placed in a canalside graveyard. The scenery improved on a long pound through a wood of mixed trees towards the junction with the Coventry canal at Fradley, where old houses lined the waterfront.

After dropping through seven locks, the waterway at Alrewas wound pleasantly through this sleepy village, under several bridges, and we tied opposite an old house in a spacious garden, a peaceful scene until a surprising assortment of noisy ducks arrived and the neighbouring church started a two-hour bell-ringing practice. On Sunday morning the peal started at 8 a.m. and went on throughout much of the day, though at least the bell-ringers were skilled and had an extensive repertoire.

Being only a few hours' cruising from the north–south dividing point on the river Trent, I rang Canalphone and heard that BWB were shutting Weedon aqueduct for an unspecified period to carry out emergency work. We could not be certain of returning to London down the Grand Union. Once again, we had to make a radical change of plan: from the Leicester arm at Norton junction, we would have to switch across country to the Oxford canal, thence down the Thames to Brentford and back up the Grand Union through London to Rickmansworth.

While the change of route was appealing and interesting, the problem was compounded by the need to pass through Shepperton lock, which was being closed by Thames Water Authority on 28 October; also, we had to obtain a short-term licence from TWA, not easily accomplished without regular mail. From Alrewas to our destined mooring there were 265 miles and 174 locks; allowing time-in-hand for possible delays and breakdowns, it meant that we had to set a fairly steady daily rate of progress.

The river Trent splayed into numerous streams in the flood meadows below Alrewas (the name apparently derived from Alder Wash on account of the abundance of alder trees, used for basket-weaving, that once grew in the often flooded valley) and merged with the canal under a series of wooden trestle bridges where it was overlooked by a little isolated fourteenth-century church at Wychnor.

This lazy rural scene did not survive for long as the river departed over a weir and the canal continued parallel with the hectic A35 to Burton-on-Trent, where we felt that we could have become intoxicated from the heavy vapours emitted by the many breweries in this greatest of beer-producing towns. I was relieved to learn that the water that had made Burton beers so renowned was not taken from the river, but drawn from artesian wells.

After curving through Shardlow, once a busy transhipment point, the canal again joined forces with the Trent, grown into a fully fledged river, and continued through an active leisure-boating centre at Long Eaton and Sawley. Beyond there was a crossroads formed by the Erewash canal (leading to D. H. Lawrence's Eastwood) and the river Soar, where we were heading.

I felt a spontaneous urge to have just a taste of the full river Trent, partly to postpone if only for a few hours the final turn back towards London, partly to enjoy the glorious hot September sunshine, such as we had not experienced during the summer. Turning left into Cranfleet cut and dropping through a lock, we entered a further wide reach of river and *Frederick* surged in the fine deep water, charging as far as the outskirts of Nottingham before, finally, swinging back to the south.

A day later we entered the river Soar, where the lower part was being torn apart by earth-moving machines building new flood-protection banks, and we came up to the second lock behind another boat; clasping with its talons a stand on the roof, a bird of prey was chained, eagerly surveying its surroundings.

'A three-month-old kestrel,' its owner explained, taking it on to his gloved hand so that I could admire its rich tawny shades of plumage. The savagely hooked bird studied me intently through jet-black hooded eyes. 'It lives on day-old chicks – the whole thing,' he continued. 'As a bird of prey, it needs both flesh and bones, otherwise the food passes through too quickly; in fact, I have to add cotton wool to the diet to help its digestion. They're becoming very popular around these parts.'

Another experience was awaiting us on our way to Leicester. Beyond Mountsorrel – where on a lovely meadow mooring the noise of the main road was obliterated by a cascading weir – I saw a seventy-foot narrowboat pull out of a wharf, make a rapid turn and pick up a butty on the move. Tagging along behind them, we reached Thurmaston lock, where a pair of breasted boats was descending, so heavily loaded that the gunnels barely cleared the water.

Slipping away from the lock, sensuously deep in the water, they recalled so many of the photographs of the canals when all boats were carrying loads, an entirely different perspective from surviving traditional craft which sit high on the water like an unloaded ship in port. In nearly eighteen months, they were the first pair of traditional boats that we had seen at work.

The crew of the empty boats that we were following adopted the traditional practice in ascending the lock of part-opening top paddles to speed up the process of shutting the bottom gates.

'We make this trip, carrying gravel, through one lock five times a day (in good conditions, six times), fifty weeks of the year, come flood or drought, with only two weeks off at Christmas,' one of them told me.

The working boats had slowed our progress and, for once, we had to set ourselves a target, Leicester marina, where we had arranged to leave *Frederick* for two days while we went to London to discuss final departure arrangements with our tenant. We arrived in the gathering dusk, and no one seemed to expect us. 'Jack, he's the nightwatchman, he'll look after you,' said the lady in charge as she departed from the office by car.

We met an upright and bright-blue-eyed man, perhaps in his late sixties. He was Jack Monk, in fact aged eighty-two, one of the last and best-known Number Ones, who had worked boats all his life until the traffic failed.

'Aye, I used to work Brentford to Brummagem in fifty-six hours,' he confirmed, 'but you couldn't do it now, not under these conditions – lucky to make it in a few days and that'd be in an unloaded boat.'

We told him that we were heading back to London down the Thames and wondered about the state of the river in the autumn. It fired a series of memories for him.

'We 'ad to keep going in those days, y'know, if you 'ad a load. It didn't matter if it was flooding or not,' he recalled. 'There was this time, I remember, when we was coming to Sonning bridge with a pair, deep in the water. If you know it, there's only one low narrer arch to go through. I tried to slow, but the blasted butty started to go by the motor on the flood, so's there was no choice, we had to shoot the arch, 'oping it was the right one. We got thru', all right, but I reckon there's still some missing parts of that bridge.'

After returning from our brief visit to London, we passed through Saddington tunnel, quite short at 880 yards, yet one of the most crooked on the system and reputedly the home of bats, though we saw none. We reached the bottom of the Foxton flight, an ascent of seventy-five feet by means of two clusters of staircase locks separated by a short middle pound – in a way, the longest staircase in England. From the bottom lock it looked almost vertical, but we had no opportunity to ponder on it; the keeper told us that the lower half was free to enter and, after passing a descending boat in the middle, we had accomplished ten locks to the summit in fifty minutes. Why did they not build more flights like this?

Oddly enough, there should have been a second parallel flight of locks built at Foxton to reduce the pressure of demand on this narrowbeam flight. Instead, inventive genius took over and in 1900 an inclined plane was constructed to by-pass the flight with boats transferred into water containers, balanced one against another, and lifted up the hillside on rails. It was a marvellous conception which never worked successfully and was abandoned after eleven years, probably because of inadequate power from the pump-house which, when we saw it, was being restored as an information centre. The remains of the wide rail tracks that carried the caissons containing boats could be discerned on the far side of the hill from the top lock.

We continued through rolling Leicestershire countryside, alternating between pastures and arable land already showing the green shoots of winter corn, sown after the summer's crop. On a sunny October day, the canalside was brilliant with scarlet berries of hips and haws, and damson-blue sloes, startling on bare thorn branches; the hedges were heavy still with succulent, deep-purple clusters of elderberries, with a few surviving blackberries.

At Yelverton, close to Market Harborough, we tied overnight and began to wonder about these luscious, unclaimed fruits of autumn. We looked up an old recipe for 'Hedgerow Jam', which included hazel nuts, walked along the towing-path and picked just enough of each variety to make a preserve which combined all the golden, burnt flavours of autumn.

Two more tunnels at Husbands Bosworth and Crick, then the descent of six locks at Watford and we had arrived back at Norton junction, almost one year after last passing it on our way to Lapworth. Now, instead of turning south on to the Grand Union as originally intended, we went through the kink of Braunston tunnel on our way to the Oxford canal.

At Calcutt, we paused to talk with the boatyard about ways of improving *Frederick*'s heating for another winter living on board, and then ascended Napton flight in such grey, misty weather that we could barely discern the white sails of the restored windmill on the hill behind. We spent about four hours crossing the flat Oxford summit, the canal winding tortuously around the smallest of hills, at places almost returning in a loop to its starting-point and at Fenny Compton passing through a narrow defile, once a tunnel and now simply a cutting. At Claydon, the canal started to drop through eight locks as the countryside became softer and more interesting, finally reaching Cropredy, a village built around the canal in Oxfordshire stone and thatch.

Rosemary and Simon Grant – who had come to see us over the previous winter at Lapworth and visited the Other Place at Stratford with us – gave us a stupendous meal, both of them being perfection-ist cooks, in their comfortable cottage near the Red Lion in a street leading up from the canal. The next morning, no one was in a fit state to do any serious boating, but they came out quite early to see us on our way down the Oxford canal.

We were glad to pass through the lock in the centre of Banbury at a quiet time, since it had an awkward exit with a wooden road-bridge that had to be lifted; moreover, the town had acquired a dubious reputation among boaters for vandalism. The slender, high spire of King's Sutton took over the skyline, back in open country, as we approached the deepest lock, twelve feet, at Sommerton; further on at Upper Heyford, awesome black supersonic jets screamed in rapid succession from the runway immediately above the canal, then seemed to swoop low over *Frederick* as though using the boat for target practice.

Below the Rock of Gibraltar pub, we passed through another lock into the river Cherwell, where the water level was so low that a boat was stranded in the shallows. Despite our efforts to raise it by opening the sluices, it remained firmly entrenched and we motored down the meandering river between willows to the curious wide weir lock above Shipton-on-Cherwell.

We arrived back in Thrupp to tie overnight – the place where we had started out on our voyage eighteen months earlier. It brought back a flood of memories of the three weeks that we had spent bringing car-loads of possessions and furnishings from London and fitting out the boat.

Two hours from Thrupp, we turned off the canal through a stop-lock and into Duke's Cut, leading to a wide reach of the Thames. It was tempting – but we could not spare the three or four days it would have taken – to swing upstream to the head of navigation at the lovely Cotswolds village of Lechlade, directly linked to the Severn until the canal was closed in 1927.

Instead, we turned left into King's, the last of the series of upper Thames locks worked manually by resident keepers pushing against the near beam and moving the far one with a long shaft, a perfect act of weight-balancing. A mile downstream at Godstow, the lock had been mechanised (like all those between here and Teddington) so that the keeper, looking like a naval officer in double-breasted brass-buttoned uniform and white topped cap, only had to flick levers.

The dreaming spires of Oxford could be discerned across the great expanse of Port Meadow, common land where individuals grazed their horses, roaming in wild stomping herds like a scene from a Western film. In the far corner we passed Medley Boat Station, where *Hanover* had been moored for eighteen months, and swept down a fast narrow section of river, under Folly bridge into the heart of the city.

We tied on one of the finest moorings in the country opposite Christ Church meadows, feeling privileged to enjoy a view that no money could buy: a skyline of collegiate history stretching from Tom Tower, the cathedral and Merton's pinnacles to Magdelen's elegant tower.

Rowing seemed to be the predominant occupation of students, with eights, fours and sculls battling for space and narrowly avoiding collision. The air resounded with the exhortations of invective – screaming coaches treating their crews like galley slaves, regardless that many were pretty young girls. They were out again at first light, about 7 a.m., next morning, while the towing-path thundered with joggers. It was positively exhausting just hearing all this youthful energy being spent.

The sun was peering through a low layer of mist cushioning the river as we set out downstream. With few other boats on the move we made fast progress, each lock being opened as we started to approach, whereas in summer we could have idled for thirty minutes or longer while boats were packed into locks. Before lunch, the characteristic clump of beeches on top of perfectly rounded Sinodun hill came into sight, and we reached Dorchester in half a day, less than half the time we would have reckoned at peak season.

We tied in a meadow and wandered into the narrow main street, freed from traffic by a recently opened by-pass, reminded by the seventeenth-century abbey that this had been the cathedral city of Wessex. We took a favourite walk along the line of Iron Age earthworks, which could have been a canal cut, crossed Day's Lock and climbed the steep hill to the clump of trees surrounded by the foundations of a Saxon fort. The whole of Oxfordshire was spread out as a patchwork beneath us.

The last week of October turned into an Indian summer as we progressed rapidly down the Thames, the thickly wooded hillsides at Goring and Sonning burnished by the sun into a glowing panorama of golden browns, yellows and reds. The scene was repeated, perhaps more dramatically, at Cliveden, where we had a glimpse, above the high woods, of the magnificent, once scandalous mansion. We tied overnight at Henley at the place where the stewards' enclosure would be erected for the Royal Regatta, and gasped constantly at the scale and luxuriousness of riverside houses, set in immaculate gardens, around Maidenhead and Bray. We decided that, next summer, we would have to return to enjoy a superb mooring at Cookham, and we had lunch at Windsor with an uninterrupted view of the castle. We reflected that royalty did not have the same free opportunity that we were enjoying to see so many beautiful sights in brilliant weather on a river which we had almost to ourselves, and decided that October was definitely the best time of year to cruise along the Thames.

We passed through Shepperton lock – just one and a half hours before it was scheduled to be closed for repairs – and the towing-path was alive with Sunday afternoon strollers, basking in late autumn sun. We tied below the lock and walked through the outskirts of Weybridge to the bottom lock of the river Wey to revive memories of our first serious boating, when we had acquired *Hanover* one frosty January day, at Godalming, the navigational head of the river. We promised ourselves a more leisurely return visit next year to the peaceful, tree-lined, smoothly flowing waterway.

Dry leaves pattered on the roof like raindrops overnight and November-grey drabness tinged the next morning. A chill wind had risen by the time we reached Teddington in the evening and tied above the last lock of the non-tidal Thames where, since it was a point of entry to the country, posters reminded boaters that the importing of animals was prohibited in order to reduce the risk of rabies.

Brentford lock from the Thames into the Grand Union opened two hours either side of high tide, and I had reckoned from my previous experience in *Hanover* that it took about one and a half hours to cover this section. At Teddington, high tide was expected at 7 a.m. and, during the past day or so, I had been trying to establish whether there would be sufficient daylight to steer down the river.

After a restless night of worrying, the alarm woke us at 5.45. I peered out of the window into pitch darkness. As we breakfasted, forlorn and bedraggled, dawn began to glimmer and in bleak light at 6.50 a.m. I started the engine, our nerves more ragged about this final stage of the return to London than the potential hazards of the tidal river.

A fierce wind was blowing across the cut as we edged towards the lock. It was closed, and the hooter failed to raise the keeper. Suddenly *Frederick* was caught by the cross wind and blown sideways along the narrow channel, already reduced in width by lines of moored boats. Swinging dangerously towards them, I realised that there was no option but to turn around, away from the lock. Crashing into a clear bank, we managed to motor back to the open river, wind across the top of the weir and return towards the lock, by now open. We had lost thirty precious minutes of the two hours needed to reach Brentford.

With the current behind us, putting on full speed, we swept past Twickenham. Richmond Hill, Kew Gardens and Syon Park were left behind as we approached the secluded entrance to Brentford, angled towards up-river traffic. Going downstream, then turning back against the current, we entered the safety of the channel and saw that one of the pair of locks was ready. The friendly keeper gave us a warm welcome as we entered the safety of the lock; it was a relief to return to the informal atmosphere of the canals after the somewhat remote grandeur of the Thames.

We shared the Hanwell flight of six locks with a delightful, though somewhat inexperienced, young couple who left me plenty of work in closing gates and shutting paddles, which I enjoyed after the lazy days of keeper-run locks on the Thames.

After nine hours of travelling since the tricky dawn start, in extremely cold, windy conditions, we arrived thankfully below the Shovel pub at Uxbridge. Across a small park, we could see slow-moving rush-hour traffic under orange sodium lights, telling us that we were back again in London after eighteen months of travelling in the country.

From Brentford to Uxbridge, we had passed through mile after mile of dense housing and factories. The next morning, leaving the M40 behind, the Grand Union began to climb through smart black and white locks into the rural valley of the river Colne, opening on either side to a series of flooded gravel pits, now turned into leisure and nature reserve lakes, from Harefield to Rickmansworth.

We tied below Black Jack's lock. Opposite, sheep were grazing on pastures rising steeply above waterside willows; beyond the towing-path, a white dinghy with blue sails was skimming among little islands with sparse trees like a classic Japanese painting. We strolled through water gardens and trees to Copper Mill lock, where a line of terraced houses had been lovingly restored and ducks were swimming contentedly, and thought back to five years ago when we had brought *Hanover* from the Wey on to the Grand Union, knowing nothing about it.

We were left with two frantic days of preparing for a change-around, once again, in our way of life: first catching the London underground to Paddington, thence by train to Warwick, picking up the car that we had not seen for four months and had left in the safe-keeping of Eric and Ruth, catching up with their news since they moved to the Saltisford mooring, and driving (now a strange experience) back to London.

The dreaded morning, finally, had arrived. From the day that we had left Stourport, setting out on the long way back, there had been a cloud growing larger and darker all the time in the back of our minds that not even the splendid golden October weather had been able to banish. At 8 a.m., the first winter frost was glistening on the ground, the car was iced, and it was so cold that I had to relight the fire to warm our hands. Lynda slipped on the icy surface, nastily damaging a leg so that she was restricted in her movements.

The hour chimed when our travelling home would be transmogrified into a land-based house. Too busy to dwell on our emotions, the car was packed to the roof with clothing, linen, pictures, china and other possessions, and we set out along the rough country lane, on to the urban by-pass, joining the ever-increasing body of traffic on the Western Avenue link with the M40.

The countryside fell away behind us, taken over by factories and housing estates, then by high-rise blocks and roads so thick on the ground that all sight of nature was excluded. As the elevated section of the motorway rose on concrete stanchions above the level of ordinary houses, I began to wonder how people could survive in these surroundings. In the pit of my stomach was the kind of sick feeling that I remembered from the first day at school and National Service and starting a new job.

Coming off the elevated flyover at Paddington and down into the inevitable traffic jam on the Euston Road, hounded by vehicles on either side, we shunted bumper-to-bumper into the thick of King's Cross, crawled up the hill to the Angel and around the corner into the chaos of Upper Street, Islington. Arriving back at the house that we had occupied until eighteen months ago, we had to plunge into all the problems that occur when one person moves out and another moves in: trials and tribulations with the removals people, and the final settling of contracts.

We were living back in a house and our eighteen months of freedom on the waterways seemed to drain away in about as many minutes; we had much more space and the comforts of a new architect-designed building, yet we found it difficult to settle down within the relatively spacious four walls. The outside noise of cars being started in the morning and voices in the street were alien, beneath the house we could detect the passing rumble of underground trains, occasionally we could hear the shrill claxon of the emergency services. We had become accustomed to entirely different sounds: ducks quacking and cattle bellowing, the cries of geese in flight, the eerie call of a reed warbler and the splashing movement of another boat passing our mooring.

Only a few minutes' walk away the Regent's canal passed through Islington tunnel, 960 yards long, opened in 1816 and still going strong. From there, the Grand Union climbed to the summit at Tring, dropped to Marsworth and Aylesbury, passed through Blisworth to the junction with the Nene and continued on to Braunston where it divided, one way to the Trent and Mersey, the Caldon and Macclesfield, the other to Hatton, Lapworth, Stratford and along the Avon and Severn to Sharpness. We had been to the points of the network furthest east, north-west and south-west.

As we tried to settle back into London life, we realised that we had to make some decisions about our future. We had found that there is another England that remains alive and well outside the boundaries of frenetic urban living. We had accomplished much of what we set out to do, even though we had not been to York as hoped. First, we needed a period of readjustment to sort out the problems of house and work. Then, we felt certain that we would return to the quieter ways of the canals, revive memories and explore new routes. There is something elusive and compelling about the waterways that urges you back and back again.

A Selected List of Non-Fiction Available from Mandarin Books

While every effort is made to keep prices low, it is sometimes necessary to increase prices at short notice. Mandarin Paperbacks reserves the right to show new retail prices on covers which may differ from those previously advertised in the text or elsewhere.

The prices shown below were correct at the time of going to press.